BREAKING GROUND, BREAKING SILENCE

BREAKING GROUND, BREAKING SILENCE

The Story of New York's
African Burial Ground

**Joyce Hansen and
Gary McGowan**

Henry Holt and Company

New York

Henry Holt and Company, Inc.
Publishers since 1866
115 West 18th Street
New York, New York 10011

Henry Holt is a registered
trademark of Henry Holt and Company, Inc.

Published in Canada by Fitzhenry & Whiteside Ltd.,
195 Allstate Parkway, Markham, Ontario L3R 4T8.

Library of Congress Cataloging-in-Publication Data
Hansen, Joyce.
Breaking ground, breaking silence: the story of New York's African
burial ground/by Joyce Hansen and Gary McGowan.
p.   cm.
Summary: Describes the discovery and study of the African burial site
found in Manhattan in 1991, while excavating for a new building, and
what it reveals about the lives of black people in Colonial times.
1. New York (N.Y.)—Antiquities. 2. Slaves—New York (State)—
New York—History—18th century. 3. Afro-Americans—New York
(State)—New York—History—18th century. 4. Cemeteries—New
York (State)—New York—History—18th century. 5. Excavations
(Archaeology)—New York (State)—New York. [1. New York (N. Y.)—
Antiquities. 2. Afro-Americans—History. 3. Slaves—History.
4. Excavations (Archaeology)—New York (N.Y.)] I. McGowan, Gary.
II. Title.
F128.39.H36 1997   305.5'67'0974709034—dc21   97-19105

ISBN 0-8050-5012-4
First Edition—1998
Printed in the United States of America on acid-free paper. ∞
10 9 8 7 6 5 4 3 2 1

We would like to acknowledge Cheryl LaRoche for her scholarship,
support, and friendship
and Miriam Francis for sharing her feelings and her insights in
respecting the memories and lives of her ancestors.

Special thanks to Cynthia Copeland, museum educator
for outreach, the New-York Historical Society,
for her invaluable help on this project.

Special thanks also to Roger Taylor for
his insights and motivation in the
creation of this book.

—the authors

To my loving wife, Mary Alice, for all her love and support
and to my wonderful sons, Adam and Noah.

—Gary McGowan

In memory of my father, Austin V. Hansen, Sr.,
Photographer and Historian,
January 28, 1910, to January 23, 1996.
Time passes, but love endures.

—Joyce Hansen

CONTENTS

FOREWORD

Cemeteries and burial grounds naturally bring to mind thoughts of death, loss, endings, the unknown, silence. The archaeologist believes that in the midst of death there is life—not conscious life as we know it—but the "stuff" of life, the fragments, remnants and pieces of our human existence that evoke a people and a culture, a time and a place.

The rediscovery of the African Burial Ground in New York City, the oldest known cemetery for people of African descent in the nation, offered archaeologists a unique opportunity to break the silence of a people whose voices and history had been suppressed. Sifting through hundreds of graves and analyzing the tiniest fragment of pottery, a misshapen nail, a child's earbob and countless other artifacts, the archaeologists slowly, carefully and painstakingly began to re-create a little known past. Their work enabled a people who had no opportunity to leave us either a written or oral history to "tell" us who they were, what was important to them, what they believed, and how they lived. Blending scientific inquiry with historical research, the men and women who are still analyzing and studying the artifacts from the burial ground also bring their own hearts and instincts to the work, for the archaeologist is not only a scientist, but an artist as well. There are times when answers to questions about the past come not only from historical and scientific evidence, but from the heart and the imagination of the researcher.

We hope that the story we have told and the efforts of the women and men who continue to reclaim this lost history will challenge young people to seriously consider archaeological research as an exciting and rewarding career. The important work of understanding our collective past continues, and needs young men and women who are empathetic to the cultures and people they study—who understand that what we learn about the past helps us to understand who we are now.

BREAKING GROUND, BREAKING SILENCE

CHAPTER 1

DIGGING DOWN TO STERILE GROUND

September 30, 1991, was a breezy and sunny day in New York City, with a little nip in the air—a reminder that winter was on its way. Cranes picked up chunks of rubble, while dump trucks and backhoes whizzed and pounded. Construction workers, in their orange hard hats swarmed like a colony of ants throughout the construction site that included Broadway, Duane, Elk, and Reade streets.

Just off Reade Street, another group of men and women also worked busily. They were members of the archaeological team hired by the United States government to analyze the site before a new thirty-four-story federal office building could be constructed. The excavated area exposed old gray stone walls, once the foundation for two tiny nineteenth-century streets, known as Republican and Manhattan alleys.

Excavation of the African Burial Ground site in Lower Manhattan. *Dennis Seckler, photographer. Courtesy of General Services Administration.*

The archaeological crew was aware that the site, shown on eighteenth-century city maps as the "Negroes Burying Ground," had once been a cemetery for people of African descent, paupers (poor people), and British and American prisoners of war during the American Revolution. They expected to find, if anything, about fifty burials and a few bone fragments. What else could remain after centuries of building and changes in the original landscape?

Tractors and cranes at work on burial site. *Dennis Seckler, photographer. Courtesy of General Services Administration.*

The archaeologists worked sixteen feet below the surface of the southeastern section of the construction site. They had dug down to sterile ground—a point where humans, with their buildings, streets, and walls, had not touched. It was quieter here. Honking horns and screeching sirens from the city traffic were muffled and distant. The air was still, contained, and fresh—not like the air above the surface, thick with fumes from hundreds of cars and other motor vehicles.

The earth here was different, too. A wet, blood-red clay (alluvial clay) had been deposited throughout this region by glaciers during the Ice Age. Hundreds of small rocks and pebbles, like those found in the woods and forests of upstate New York, peppered the ground.

As the crew carefully dug into the damp, fine, silty alluvial clay, tiny particles began to seep into their clothes and the creases of their skin and body. If there was a heavy downpour of rain while they worked in this soil, the workers could begin to sink; if the ground became unstable, holes could fill up and the earth cave in.

While they dug, it became apparent that there were graves here that had been underneath this bustling part of the city for two centuries or more.

At 10:00 A.M. one team member noticed a dark outline in the earth. Since the clay was soft, it was fairly easy to dig around the outline. Using a trowel similar to a gardening tool, the team meticulously scraped away the dirt. One of them spotted a large, bright brown, oddly misshapen nail, nothing like the nails we are accustomed to seeing today.

After being buried in the earth and exposed to the elements, this nail had undergone a process called oxidation. Oxygen, salt, water, and other chemicals had corroded the metal, causing it to expand from the inside out. Thus the nail had not only enlarged in spots, but twisted like a bloated overgrown worm.

Lying on their stomachs, separated from the moist, rocky earth only by thick plywood boards, flattened boxes, and a protective covering, the team slowed down the pace of their work. What might look like an old useless object was an important discovery. The nail might have come from a colonial coffin. Perhaps they had discovered a burial site.

Using a dental pick, a soft brush, and a rubber aspirator (often used

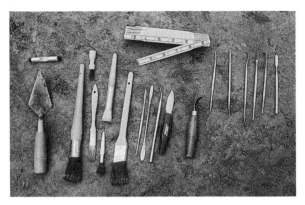

Archaeologists use many common tools to excavate the fragile remains and artifacts found in historic burial sites. The tools pictured above were used in the African Burial Ground excavations. They are (from left to right): trowel, aspirator, dental picks, tape measure. *Dennis Seckler, photographer. Courtesy of General Services Administration.*

as a baby's ear syringe) the excavators spent the rest of that day carefully removing the soil around the outline. For the next two and a half days they painstakingly pecked, pushed, and gently blew away the earth around the outline until they saw a dark stain.

They were correct about the nail, for a coffin lid was emerging. As the crew removed a rectangular, uniform portion of earth, a row of similar nails began to appear. The hexagonal shape of a casket could be made out. It appeared to be fairly typical for the eighteenth century—a modest pine or cedar coffin. The lid had melded almost completely into the red earth and the coffin had turned the dirt, with which it blended, a dark brown color, rich with the tannic acid found in wood bark.

Almost completely deteriorated, and as delicate as old parchment, the lid was only a quarter of an inch thick. The archaeologists collected tiny fibers from what remained of the wood.

For hours they brushed and peeled the lid away, hoping to find some skeletal remains. This was the most crucial part of the excavation. If the archaeologists weren't careful with their trowels and brushes, they might accidentally change the appearance of any remaining bone fragments, which could lead to false interpretations when the bones were studied and analyzed. For example, damage to the bone during a dig could falsely be interpreted as a wound, disease, or fracture from a previous injury.

The archaeologists didn't think, though, that they would find much. As they continued to brush away the soil, they realized that the weight of the earth above had caused the left side of the coffin to buckle and cave in, probably destroying the skeleton inside.

The excavation was completed by October 1. As the sun was setting and the autumn temperature dipped down to forty degrees, they finally reached the burial. The crew gazed in amazement. Instead of pieces of bone, eroded and destroyed by time, they saw a complete skeleton, face up with its arms at its sides.

Miraculously there was no serious damage, even though the water table was high here. (The water table is the level below which the ground is saturated with water.) The skeletal remains of this early New Yorker were slowly becoming part of the red earth. The remains were wet and gelatinous—almost the consistency of butter—yet the skeleton was completely intact and in remarkably good condition.

As the crew packed up and prepared to leave, it was clear to them

Burial #6, an adult male, was the first completely intact skeleton discovered during the excavation. *Dennis Seckler, photographer. Courtesy of General Services Administration.*

that this well-preserved skeleton under the streets of lower Manhattan was one of the most important archaeological discoveries of our time.

What they did not know as yet was how much spiritual, cultural, historical, and archaeological treasure Republican Alley and Manhattan Alley would yield.

CHAPTER 2

GROUND TRUTH

The following morning the archaeologists returned to the burial for the next phase of their work. They had to clean away the moist alluvial clay that was practically glued to the skeleton, now called Burial #6. Using dental picks, aspirators, and small brushes, most of the dirt was removed from the surface of the bone.

Absorbing the soil's moisture, the bones had turned soft and spongy. If not cleaned and allowed to properly dry, they would crumble like pieces of rotted wood.

When cleaning skeletal remains, the thorax or chest cavity is a critical area, for often it contains vital organic material. Soils taken from around the thorax can be analyzed to help find out which diseases were present in the body when the person died, or what the person ate as a last meal.

A member of the archaeological crew carefully excavating the remains. *Dennis Seckler, photographer. Courtesy of General Services Administration.*

Another member of the archaeological crew evaluates a burial before it is exhumed. She is noting the orientation of the skeleton (many of the skeletons faced east), and the condition of the remains. She will also note whether there are artifacts in the burial and where they lie within the coffin. The positions of artifacts provide important information. *Dennis Seckler, photographer. Courtesy of General Services Administration.*

Osteologists can examine and measure skulls and pelvic bones to determine if an individual is male or female.

Soils taken from the chest cavity usually yield seeds and food particles. These materials are extracted by sifting the soils through screens immersed in water. This process is called floatation.

As the earth was cleared away from this important middle section of the burial's body, nine small objects were found in a line down the chest. Two larger objects were found in the tailbone area. Not only had the archaeologists discovered a well-preserved skeleton, but there were possible artifacts as well.

That afternoon, as the skeleton dried, a team of osteologists, or bone scientists, arrived at the site. They began to analyze the skeleton in order to determine the age, sex, and race of the individual in Burial #6.

The osteologists concluded that Burial #6 was either an African or African-American man, thirty to forty years old and five feet eleven inches tall. The archaeological team could see that the objects lying in a line down his torso were buttons. The two large objects near his tailbone area were buttons as well, suggesting that he may have been wearing a long coat.

Thin metal pins in and
around his head area indicate that he had been
wrapped in a winding-sheet,
or shroud—a cloth substi-
tuted for clothing when
burying the dead; however,
as the buttons show, he may
have been wearing clothing.
(The archaeologists did not
expect to recover cloth or
material in the wet and
marshy environment of the
burial ground, where fabrics
such as cotton, linen, and
wool would rapidly decom-
pose.)

An iron pellet, most likely
an eighteenth-century bullet, was also found in the

Brass shroud pin from one of the burials. In the eighteenth century, the deceased were often buried in a cloth
called a shroud or winding sheet. The pins held the cloth
together. *Joshua Nefsky, photographer. Courtesy of
General Services Administration.*

The shroud pin near the skull indicates that the individ-
ual was wrapped in a shroud from head to foot. *Dennis
Seckler, photographer. Courtesy of General Services
Administration.*

grave. The archaeological crew removed the buttons and other artifacts and took them to the Foley Square Laboratory, not far from the
excavation site. The skeletal remains would be taken to another laboratory for further study.

Surrounded by microscopes, slides, file cabinets, and books, the
archaeological team began the exciting work of investigating the artifacts from Burial #6. There could be a wealth of cultural information
in the eroded, damaged items.

These artifacts might provide what archaeologists call "ground
truth." When a people and their culture have been written about and
distorted by those who oppress them, artifacts found in burials are

often the only way for archaeologists to gain a true idea of the people's culture and to either verify or dispute what had already been written about them. In a sense, it is as though people who have been written out of history have found a way to tell us about themselves through the objects buried with them.

In the days that followed, the team would try to find out what the artifacts were made of, where and when they were manufactured, and, most importantly, what the objects would tell us about the deceased.

The team followed the usual steps for processing artifacts. The buttons and other articles had to be:

a. cleaned.
b. labeled, showing where the buttons, nails, etc., had been located in the burial site—their provenance. Location of an artifact can provide vital information about culture and lifestyle. For example, because the buttons in Burial #6 were found in a line down the deceased's chest, the archaeologists could safely assume that he had been wearing clothing when he was buried. When further analysis of the artifacts are carried out in the laboratory, it is important that the researchers know exactly where the objects were found.
c. stabilized and conserved in order to stop deterioration (metals are soaked in baths of water and treated with acrylic resin and other chemical agents).
d. reconstructed—fragments are pieced together.
e. analyzed—using either chemical or microscopic analysis the archaeologist will draw conclusions based on the information he or she has gathered (hypothesis). This data or information will be compared with historical documents and texts.

The archaeologists realized that of all of the artifacts discovered in Burial #6, the buttons would probably provide important cultural information. Using a dental pick, they cleaned the buttons under a microscope so that they did not inadvertently erase or smudge patterns and designs within the fragile object.

After the buttons were cleaned, the scientists realized that three of them were gilded (covered with gold). The other buttons were made out of pewter. Damaged by years of erosion, they looked small, hard, and leaflike. However, the anchor and rope insignia of the British Navy was clearly visible.

A large brass button, approximately the size of a fifty-cent piece, was so badly deteriorated that even after cleaning, they could not tell whether there was any decoration on the button. Patterns and designs are like messages providing possible information about when and where an artifact was made.

Brass button with gold overlay from Burial #6, used by British Navy. *Joshua Nefsky, photographer. Courtesy of General Services Administration.*

The button was placed under the probing eye of a microscope, where raking light (shining light on an object sideways) revealed that it, too, had an anchor and rope insignia. At times, the metal artifacts were so badly corroded that X-ray machines had to be used in order to determine what was disguised by the corrosion.

After the buttons were labeled and stabilized, the team needed to find out when similar buttons were used. Studying photographs and illustrations of colonial-style buttons helped

Large brass button from Burial #6. *Joshua Nefsky, photographer. Courtesy of General Services Administration.*

the archaeologists determine that the buttons were the kind worn by British sailors during the American Revolution. A picture was emerging; the team began to form a hypothesis.

Perhaps the deceased had been a sailor buried in uniform and wrapped in a shroud, according to military custom. He might have been one of the thousands of African Americans enlisted in the British Navy. This was an amazing discovery. A black man in British military uniform, dating back to the American Revolution, buried in the manner accorded a soldier. Yet, the body, when found, was facing east, a burial custom of many people of African descent in the eighteenth and nineteenth centuries.

Burial #6 was just the beginning. There would be more discoveries as the ground opened up like an ancient history book. Over the next ten months, the team would repeat many times the same careful process of excavation that they had used to exhume Burial #6.

Instead of the fifty burials they expected, the team excavated more than four hundred graves.

They found burials of young children and teenagers, of old people and people in their prime. One burial contained the remains of a

After the skeletal remains were excavated, further cleaning was carried out at the Howard University Laboratory. Many of the remains were extremely fragile and it was necessary to keep some of the soil around the bones after they were removed from the grave in order to protect them. This process is called *pedestalling. Cheryl LaRoche, photographer. Courtesy of photographer.*

mother and child, another the remains of a woman still adorned with beads around her waist and wrists. Another burial yielded a woman with a musket ball in her ribcage.

The archaeologists found artifacts such as beads, buttons, coins, rings, coral fragments, shroud pins, a child's earbob, tobacco pipes, nails, and coffin handles. They closely analyzed every item, poring over the smallest detail in order to find out how eighteenth-century black New Yorkers lived and what their world was like.

Child's sterling silver earbob. These were commonly traded among Native Americans and may have been traded among the African population as well. The child may possibly have been part Native American and part African. *Paul Reckner, photographer. Courtesy of General Services Administration.*

Eventually, the archaeological team in New York City and the anthropologists at the Howard University Biological Anthropology Laboratory in Washington, D.C., began to recreate a world long gone. A people who had no voice when they were living, and who had left no written records, would at last have their stories told.

The history of people of African descent living in colonial New York City could no longer be hidden underground.

CHAPTER 3

THE LAY OF THE LAND

The African Burial Ground is located in Manhattan's civic center near the southern end of the island. In the eighteenth century it covered six acres of land, including present-day Duane Street on the north, Chambers Street on the south, Centre Street on the east, and Broadway on the west. Only the archaeologists who had dug down to where the soil had changed to the blood-red alluvial clay of an earlier period could imagine that these busy streets, now crammed with courthouses, buildings, parking lots, stores, and restaurants were once a tapestry of marshes, ponds, streams, meadows, and hills. At first there was no burial ground here either, only a deep ravine descending from the surrounding hills, and a large freshwater pond. The meadows lay like soft green brushstrokes beside clear streams that emptied into the two rivers that flanked the island. The ponds and streams teemed with shellfish, eel, shad, and possibly salmon. Deer, rabbits, birds, waterfowl, and other game thrived in the island's swamps and woodlands. Willow, cedar, oak, and fruit trees provided food and shade for the people who lived here, the Manhattans. (In various texts, they are referred to as Manhattes, Manatthans, Manates.) The island was blessed with nature's gifts.

Then, in 1609, Henry Hudson explored the North American coast. He'd been hired by the Dutch East India Company of Holland to find a quick way

A village of the Manhattans prior to Dutch occupation, as depicted in David T. Valentine's *Manual of the Corporation Council, City of NY*, 1858. Valentine commissioned artists to create lithographs based on images, pictures, and maps of historic New York. The images in Valentine's manuals are reconstructions of historical places and events. They were not drawn in the time and place they depict. *Courtesy of New-York Historical Society.*

to reach the East and its riches. The Dutch merchants were mainly interested in trade. They established a small post in 1613 near present-day Albany, New York, where they bartered with the Native Americans for furs for a short period. By 1620, however, Dutch businessmen became interested in the rich lands across the Atlantic and formed the Dutch West India Company.

The company outfitted a ship and in 1623 sent thirty families, along with fur traders and adventurers, to establish the province of New Netherland along the coastal areas that Henry Hudson had spotted in his explorations. Some of the settlers went to the north and the old fur-trading post, while a few others came to the southern tip of the island.

Henry Hudson meeting Native Americans, as depicted in Phelps Stokes's *The Iconography of Manhattan Island, 1498–1909*, volume 1. Stokes brought together preexisting images of historical New York; thus, the majority of the images in Stokes were drawn closer to the time of the events they depict than the images in Valentine's manuals. The end result was a six-volume collection, published between 1915 and 1928.

Two years after they arrived, in 1626, a ship from Holland sailed into the harbor, bringing Peter Minuit to govern the colony. Governor Minuit purchased the island from the Manhattans for sixty guilders' (twenty-four dollars') worth of merchandise and named the settlement New Amsterdam; however the Manhattans didn't think that their transaction meant that they'd sold the land to the Dutch. They thought that they were agreeing to share the land with the colonists. Perhaps, according to their way of thinking, land was like the sun or the air, belonging to everyone.

During the same year, 1626, eleven African men sailed into the harbor on one of the Dutch West India Company's ships. It's not known exactly how the company acquired these men. Maybe they had been seamen on board a ship captured by the Dutch West India Company, or perhaps they had been part of a slave cargo on a Spanish or French ship. They might have come from one of the plantations in Brazil or in the Caribbean, where the Dutch West India Company imported enslaved Africans and amassed its great wealth through the African slave trade.

The names of only four of the men are known: Paolo d'Angola,

In 1623 the colonists used enslaved Africans to help them
build Dutch New Amster-
dam. *Photograph from Stokes,*
Iconography, *volume 1.*

Simon Congo, Anthony Portuguese, and John Francisco. Their sur-
names give us a clue as to their original birthplaces. For example,
Paolo may have been born in Angola and Simon in the Congo. For the
struggling colony they were a welcome source of manpower and free
labor. There was much work to do to turn this beautiful, bountiful
land into a Dutch village. A fort had to be built, land cleared, houses,
mills, and roads constructed. Ditches and canals had to be dug in order
to redirect the flow of the ponds and swampy areas, and create more
dry land with fill materials such as soil and refuse.

Farming, too, on the outskirts of the village, required strong arms
and backs. These farms supplied the food the village needed and were
crucial to its survival. When there were labor shortages, the Dutch
West India Company brought additional Africans into the colony.

By 1630, New Amsterdam, part of the Dutch province of New
Netherland, was a small village of about three hundred people, hud-
dled on the southern tip of the island. The colony didn't extend much
beyond a mile inland. Yet, there were signs of the colony's growth.

Fort Amsterdam, with a view of both rivers, was completed in 1635, and the Church of St. Nicholas, erected inside the fort, was completed by 1642. The City Tavern, near the East River, also built by 1642, housed the many seamen coming into the port; in 1653 its name would be changed to Stadt Huys, and would be used as the city hall until 1667.

As the colony grew, conflict followed. Dutch officials began to ignore the needs and rights of the Manhattans and the other Native Americans. Willem Kieft, the third governor of the colony, increasingly saw the Indians as a hindrance to the colony's expansion and wealth. Viewing them as savages whose culture and traditions deserved little respect, he refused to settle problems peaceably, and began a campaign to destroy Native American settlements.

He ordered an attack on two settlements the night of November 25, 1643. David De Vries, a Dutch adventurer and traveler, described the first attack of the night, as soldiers rowed across the Hudson River to the opposite shore. Like some of the other colonists, he was critical of the governor's actions.

> I remained that night at the Governor's, sitting up. I went and sat by the kitchen fire, when about midnight I heard a great shrieking, and I ran to the ramparts of the fort. . . . Saw nothing but firing and heard the shrieks of the savages murdered in their sleep. . . . When it was day the soldiers returned to the fort, having massacred or murdered eighty Indians . . . infants were torn from their mother's breasts . . . and miserably massacred in a manner to move a heart of stone. . . .
>
> At another place, on the same night, on Corler's Hook, forty Indians were in the same manner attacked in their sleep, and massacred. . . .[1]

Many colonists were outraged over the events of February 25th, fearing that it would be only a matter of time before Native Americans retaliated.

In the spring of 1643, their fears were realized when Native Americans burned and demolished farms and homes in the outlying areas of what are now Brooklyn, Staten Island, and the Bronx. Many settlers lost their lives as well as their farms.

As the months wore on the situation did not improve. All farming had stopped and the village was on the brink of starvation. Something had to be done.

On July 13, 1643, the governor, merchants, and military men who made up the city council, gave a free black woman, Catelina Anthony, eight acres of farmland. Domingo Anthony, who was also free and of African descent, received thirteen acres of farmland. The land deeded to Catelina and Domingo was in the outlying regions of New Amsterdam where farms had been attacked and raided. If Native Americans should attack the village and Fort Amsterdam, they would begin with the farmland just deeded to the free blacks.

By December most of Long Island and Manhattan Island had been reclaimed by the Indians. The desperate settlers, frightened and facing annihilation themselves, wrote to the authorities in Holland begging for help: "Our fields lie fallow and waste; our dwellings and other buildings are burnt . . . we are seated here in the midst of thousand of Indians . . . from whom is to be experienced neither peace nor pity. . . ."[2]

In the meantime, Kieft had his own plans. In December 1643, he granted additional ruined land to two more free black people: a woman, Marycke, and a man, Manuel Trumpeter. Trumpeter received eighteen acres of land. Their land was near Catelina Anthony's property.

Continuing to wage war, Governor Kieft refused to listen to reason.

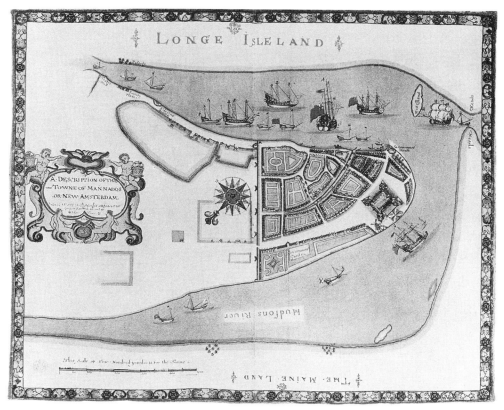

Early Dutch map of Manhattan Island shows Fort Amsterdam at the end of the island. *Photograph from Stokes*, Iconography, *volume 1.*

He asked Captain John Underhill, a British commander, to help him. Underhill had successfully cut down the Pequot tribe of Connecticut.

On about February 20, 1644, Underhill and his soldiers traveled to what is now Westchester County. They attacked an Indian settlement at night, killing hundreds of people.

Five days after the destruction of the Native American settlement, the men who sat on the Council of New Amsterdam conducted their regular meeting. Underhill's destruction of the Indian village was probably the main topic of discussion, but they had another issue to consider as well. Eleven black men, who belonged to the Dutch West

India Company, presented a petition for freedom: Paolo d'Angola, Manuel de Gerritt, Simon Congo, Anthony Portuguese, Pieter Santome, John Fort Orange, Big Manuel, Little Manuel, John Francisco, Little Antony, and Gratzia d'Angola. Several of these men had been among the first Africans brought to the colony eighteen years before.[3]

The black population of the colony had grown, for now there were women and children among them as well. The eleven men probably knew that the other blacks had been granted land, and were, therefore, encouraged to seek freedom and a land grant as well.

CHAPTER 4

A LITTLE FREEDOM

What was life like in the village in 1644, when Paolo d'Angola, Manuel de Gerritt, Simon Congo, and the others asked for their freedom?

New Amsterdam was still a small, rough settlement on the southern tip of the island. There was the fort, with its church inside, a few homes and shops, and a mill. Beside the Church of St. Nicholas inside Fort Amsterdam, there was another church and parsonage and the Dutch West India Company's brewery, warehouses, and house where the enslaved men, women, and children belonging to the company lived. Beyond the scattered buildings and homes lay the common pastures, bouweries (farms), swamps, and woodlands.

There were no schools, hospitals, or poorhouses in New Amsterdam. Enslaved people, belonging to individuals, lived in their owners' households. Couples who belonged to different owners could not live together as a family. Any children born of these unions usually lived with the mother. The child, however, belonged to neither parent, but to the mother's owner. The seeds of resistance to slavery were sown during these years. The first resisters on record in New York (then New Amsterdam) were the eleven men who petitioned the Dutch West India Company and the director of the colony, Governor Kieft, for their freedom. It was a quiet and orderly resistance, but resistance nonetheless.

Early Dutch New Amsterdam. The Dutch colonists used this romantic image of the colony to attract European settlers. The gallows pictured in the foreground conveyed the message that lawlessness would not be tolerated. However, the colony was no more than a crude settlement. *Photograph from Stokes,* Iconography, *volume 1.*

The Kolch (or Kolch-Hook) Pond. African burial grounds are often built near bodies of water. In this stylized view, the African Burial Ground (which was left out of this picture) is on the left, near the fenced-in area. *From Valentine,* Manual, *1857. Courtesy of New-York Historical Society.*

As the governor and the Council reviewed the petition they considered the fact that the men had labored many years for the Company. Their character was excellent and they had been loyal and hardworking. Most of all, the colony needed them. They were skilled, experienced workers, and since New Amsterdam still needed farmers to grow food during this time of war, the Council and the governor gave the men their freedom and a land grant with certain conditions.

The men and their wives would be freed, but their children, born and unborn, would remain enslaved, property of the Dutch West India Company. It was a bitter freedom, for their fruit, their children, would remain enslaved.

In 1650, a writer describing the colony commented on the immorality of this arrangement. "There are also . . . other Negroes in this country, some of whom have been made free for their long service, but their children have remained slaves, though it is contrary to the laws of every people that any one born of a free Christian mother should be a slave and be compelled to remain in servitude."[1]

The secretary of the province, who had a large farm outside of the tiny village, answered the charge. He said, "At present there are only three of these children who do any service. One of them is at the House of Hope [Connecticut], one at the Company's bouwery, and one with Martin Crigier, who has brought the girl up well, as everybody knows."[2] He makes no mention of the unborn children in his attempt to justify the arrangement. The children would remain slaves.

The freed families also had to pay, once a year for the rest of their lives, twenty-two bushels of corn, wheat, peas, or beans and one hog.[3] If they did not keep this part of the bargain, they would lose their land and their freedom.

The free blacks were, in reality, still bound to the Dutch West India Company, but they had some rights as "free" people. They couldn't suddenly be sold away with no regard to their attachment to loved ones. A husband, a wife, and their children could live together under one roof as a family. Most of all, they could take care of themselves. Eventually, many of these families purchased their children's freedom, as in the case of Emanuel Pietersen and his wife, Dorothy Angola. The couple petitioned the court to obtain the freedom of a boy, Anthony Angola, whom they had adopted, raised, and educated since he was a baby. Pietersen paid the Dutch West India Company three hundred guilders for Anthony's freedom.[4]

The land the freed people received was in the same wild, war-torn, outlying area of the city where Catelina Anthony and the three other blacks had been granted land a few months before. Their property was well outside of the village, north of the swamp, the common lands, and the public cow pasture. It was near, however, a deep ravine and the large freshwater pond.

Kieft did not give this land to the blacks merely out of the generosity of his heart. In case of an attack, residents in this outlying area would be struck first, giving people in the town time to organize a defense.

If there had not been a war with the Indians, most likely neither Marycke, Catelina Anthony, nor any other African would have been granted this land. For a little freedom and land Paolo d'Angola, Manuel de Gerritt, Simon Congo, and the other black men and women were willing to risk their lives. Their area became known as "land of the Blacks" or "Negroes land." It has also been called the Negro frontier and Negro Coast.

About thirty farms spanned an area that stretched from today's Chinatown up to Greenwich Village. According to one historian, "Commonly, the farms ranged in size from eight to twelve acres and consisted of thatched or wooden roof houses with some cattle, goats and sheep, a garden, and fruit trees. The more prosperous farmers might own a horse or two."[5]

These families were the beginning of a black community in the colony of New Amsterdam. This small group of pioneers was also the beginnings of a new people forged in the fires of slavery.

They could now have some semblance of freedom. For example, couples could have legal marriages, not slave marriages. The first recorded marriage of an African couple was in 1641 between Anthony van Angola and Lucie d'Angola.

Africans could attend the six Dutch churches in New Amsterdam. Forty African worshipers made up the congregation of Peter Stuyvesant's church, the Bowery Chapel.

When Paolo d'Angola and the other black men petitioned Governor Kieft for their freedom in 1644, there was no special burial ground for people of African descent. They were buried along with other villagers in the cemetery situated near the orchards and gardens of the Dutch West India Company, not far from the Hudson River. Enslaved domestic servants may have been buried in a separate area of a family plot. Burials also might have taken place in the church cemetery.

A Dutch minister wrote in 1660 that after preaching in the village of Breuckelen (Brooklyn), "The Bouwery is a place of relaxation and pleasure, whither people go from the Manhattans, for the evening

Peter Stuyvesant, last Dutch governor before the English occupation. *Photograph from Stokes*, Iconography, *volume 1.*

service. There are . . . forty Negroes, from the region of the Negro Coast, besides the household families."[6]

In this rugged little trading colony, which was actually controlled by the Dutch West India Company, a group of people of African descent —landowners, farmers, skilled laborers, and artisans—were a necessary part of the colony.

Peter Stuyvesant replaced Governor Kieft in 1647. Kieft's disastrous wars had almost ruined the colony. Stuyvesant immediately began to fortify the colony against its British neighbors, who were also grabbing land in the region. Enslaved Africans continued to trickle into the village, where their labor was needed to build a defensive wall to protect the colony from attack by British forces in 1653. The wall, extending from river to river, ran parallel to a lane that is today's Wall Street.

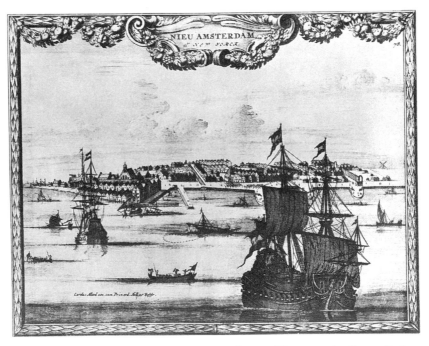

The British sail into New Amsterdam. *Photograph from Stokes, Iconography, volume 1.*

When the village could not afford to import ship carpenters and blacksmiths, African artisans did this work. Under Dutch rule, these men and women had a chance of eventually gaining their freedom. However, when the British sailed into the Port of New Amsterdam in 1664 and seized the colony, the little freedom that people like Marycke, Manuel Trumpeter, Anthony Portuguese, and the other freed blacks enjoyed would erode and virtually disappear.

CHAPTER 5

SLAVERY'S CHAINS

On August 27, 1664, when Commander Richard Nicolls sailed into the harbor of New Amsterdam with four hundred troops, the villagers did not resist. Dissatisfied with the way the colony had been run, they welcomed the new rulers. The British leaders changed the village's name to New York in honor of the Duke of York, and for most of the people life went on as usual.

Wealthy Dutch merchants and families kept their property. However, the new rulers of the colony immediately began to inquire about the land belonging to the black farmers. Peter Stuyvesant was asked to explain, and informed them in writing that the blacks had cleared

New Amsterdam became New York when the British took over the colony in 1664. Fort Amsterdam was renamed Fort George. *Photograph from Stokes,* Iconography, *volume 1*

and cultivated the three hundred acres of farmland they owned, and that the land had been given to them just as land had been given to other inhabitants of the province of New Netherlands. In other words, the freed Africans had as much right to their land as anyone else in the former Dutch province.

However, the British colonists had other plans for New York. Because of its excellent harbor, the Duke of York encouraged slave ships to land in the port of New York. Increasing numbers of enslaved people were brought into the colony to work on farms in Long Island, Staten Island, and Westchester County. As the enslaved population grew, the number of free people of African descent dwindled along with the few rights they had.

Those who were enslaved found the chains of slavery tighter than ever. Colonial rulers did not want slaves to receive religious instruction or be Christianized. Writing to his fellow ministers in Amsterdam, in 1664, Reverend Henricus Selyns reported that, "As to baptisms, the [Africans] occasionally request that we should baptize their children, but we have refused to do so. . . . They wanted nothing else than to deliver their children from bodily slavery, without striving for piety and Christian virtues. . . ."[1]

Like most parents, the enslaved Africans wanted a better life for their children. Probably many of the adults still clung to their African religions but wanted their children to be baptized and become free Christians. Under British rule, however, Christianizing enslaved people was not encouraged.

In 1699 the king of England ordered New York's governor to convert Africans and Native Americans in the colony to Christianity. The governor, Richard Coote, wrote back to the king saying that the colonists would not convert them because they might begin to entertain thoughts of freedom and the blacks were the only servants the colonists had. They feared that their slaves would ask for freedom.

In 1696 Trinity Church forbade Africans and people of African descent to be buried within city limits. *Photograph from Stokes,* Iconography, *volume 1.*

So that no slaves would be lost to Christianity, a law was passed in 1706 stating that baptism of a slave did not mean that he or she could ask to be freed.

As New Amsterdam made the transition to New York, Africans and people of African descent were increasingly restricted not only in life, but in death as well. Trinity Church, erected in 1696, ruled that "No Negro shall be buried in Trinity Churchyard."[2]

Whether they were slave or free, peo-

Lispenard's Meadows as drawn by A. Anderson, 1785. The African Burial Ground stretched from the Palisades (on left) to the Collect Pond. *From Valentine,* Manual, *1856. Courtesy of New-York Historical Society.*

ple of African descent could not be buried within the city limits. (Jews and Catholics also had to be buried outside of the city.)

African New Yorkers were allowed to bury their dead on a site near the land of the black farmers on the outskirts of the city. They might have begun using this site, near a freshwater pond and a ravine descending from the hills, as early as 1690. It was a separate place, apart from the city, undesirable land that had not been consecrated or blessed by the church. Some of it was common land, belonging to the colony, and meant to be a potter's field, a burial ground where outsiders in a village and very poor people are interred. It was a place for outcasts and a dumping ground for the refuse from the nearby pottery kilns, where ceramics were manufactured.

Yet, the African Burial Ground gave Africans and people of African descent the

One of the methods archaeologists used to determine the time period when the burial ground was in use was through *terminus post quem* and *terminus ante quem* dating of the artifacts found in the graves.

Terminus post quem
The date after which an artifact is manufactured. For example, if a coin found in a burial was minted in 1738, the burial would surely have happened after that date.

Terminus ante quem
Latest manufactured date of artifacts. For example, if shards of pottery manufactured in 1795 were found as part of the landfill covering the burial, then the date of interment would have to be prior to 1795.

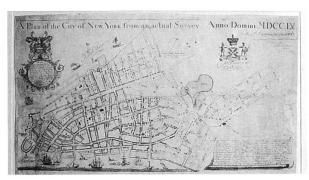

Drawn in 1754 by Thomas Maerschalck, this is the first map to show the burial ground site on the outskirts of the city. It also depicts the Palisades, or high fence, adjacent to the burial ground. The fence controlled movement in and out of the city and protected city residents from outside attack. The map also shows the presence of a freshwater pond near the burial ground. *Courtesy of New York Public Library.*

opportunity to retain an important element of their African past—funeral and burial customs. In traditional West African societies, an individual is buried with care and respect.

By 1698, there were about seven hundred people of African descent living in the city.[3] Though they came from varied backgrounds—whether they were the descendants of the old free black community dating back to the Dutch period, or enslaved men and women imported from Jamaica and other Caribbean islands, or from the West Coast of Africa—they had common African roots. Those roots were deep and strong for some, and barely there for others who had joined Christian churches, but the ties to an African past were never completely eradicated.

Many of the excavated burials indicate that, following African tradition, much care was taken in laying the indi-

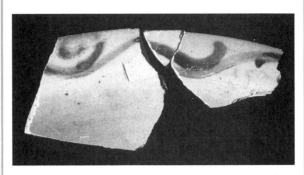

Stoneware pottery shards believed to be kiln refuse from the surrounding pottery industry that later used the burial ground as a dump. *Dennis Seckler, photographer. Courtesy of General Services Administration.*

This grave appears to have been disturbed. *Dennis Seckler, photographer. Courtesy of General Services Administration.*

The archaeologists dug through layers of kiln refuse generated by the Remmey and Crolius pottery works. Pottery fragments were strewn throughout the cemetery.

vidual to rest. Heads were buried facing east, so that when the individual sat up on Judgment Day, he or she would face the east—Jerusalem and Africa. Also following various West African traditions, funerals were held at night. During these burials Christian prayers, maybe an Ashanti prayer by an elder who remembered, and the ritual wailing for the dead could be heard among the hills of Broadway.

White people heard it, but didn't understand the sound. David Valentine, writing a "History of Broadway" in the 1850s, long after the burial ground had been closed, described it as follows:

> Beyond the Commons lay what in the earliest settlement of the town had been appropriated as a burial place for Negroes, slaves and free. It was a desolate, unappropriated spot, descending with a gentle declivity towards a ravine which led to the Kalkhook pond. The Negroes in this city were, both in the Dutch and English colonial times, a proscribed and detested race.... Many of them were native Africans, imported hither in slaveships, and retaining their native

superstitions and burial customs, among which was that of burying by night, with various mummeries and outcries. . . . The lands were unappropriated, and though within convenient distance from the city, the locality was unattractive and desolate, so that by permission the slave population were allowed to inter their dead there.[4]

This statement, though reflecting the ignorance and prejudice of the writer, confirms the cultural significance of the burial ground. The "mummeries and outcries" he'd heard about were the ritual wailing for the dead, and perhaps an Ashanti elegy:

I am an orphan, and when I recall the death of my father
    water falls from my eyes upon me.
When I recall the death of my mother, water from my eyes
    falls upon me.
We walk, we walk, O Mother Tano,
    until now we walk and it will soon be night.
It is because of the sorrow of death that we walk.[5]

One of the rare tombstones recovered at the site. Out of more than four hundred burials, only a few had grave markers. *Dennis Seckler, photographer. Courtesy of General Services Administration.*

A place meant for outcasts, the burial ground was consecrated by the prayers to God and the ancestors. It did not matter what others thought of these people of Africa. Their strength and power would come from how they viewed themselves.

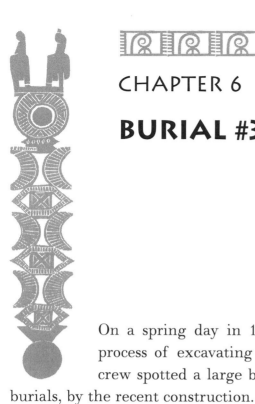

CHAPTER 6

BURIAL #340

On a spring day in 1992, the archaeologists were still in the process of excavating burials. In the midst of their work, the crew spotted a large burial pit, its dirt disturbed, like the other burials, by the recent construction.

But there was something different about the yellow, claylike soil around Burial #340. They decided to search for a coffin lid and carefully began to scrape the hard-to-remove dirt. Slowly, a gray stain began to appear. Now the archaeologists would have to be extremely careful, as they delicately scraped around it.

When the crew detected skeletal remains, they realized that the stained earth was all that was left of the coffin lid. The lid itself had melded into the soil. Like many of the others in the burial ground, this burial faced the east.

Once the dirt was entirely removed, the scientists observed tiny roundish objects around the skeleton's thigh and hip area. Except for several shroud pins and a clay pipe, no other articles were found. The archaeologists realized that the round objects might be beads. Two burials of children had been found with beads in earlier excavations. One of them had twenty-two "small black beads" around the waist and the other around the neck.[1] The remains and the articles in Burial #340 were taken to the lab for analysis. After careful study, the archaeologists confirmed what they had first suspected: the

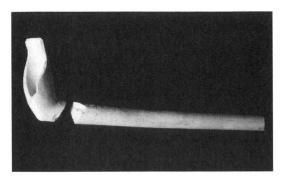 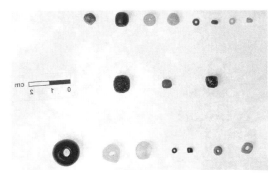

Clay pipe from Burial #340. Both women and men smoked pipes. Burying a person with his or her possessions was a custom among many African peoples. *Joshua Nefsky, photographer. Courtesy of General Services Administration.*

A variety of trade beads were found in several burials. *Doville Nelson, photographer. Courtesy of Cheryl LaRoche.*

objects were beads. One hundred forty-five beads were found in seven burials. Burial #340 yielded 111 beads, the largest amount obtained so far from a single grave.

After the archaeologists carefully analyzed the beads and researched their use among Africans and people of African descent, they then had some idea about the life and culture of this individual.

The forensic specialists, (scientists who analyze remains to determine the cause of death, the age, and the sex of the person), provided other information. They reported that Burial #340 was a woman between twenty-five and thirty years old when she died. And the shape of some of the woman's teeth had been altered. One incisor tooth had been filed in a shape resembling an hourglass. Another incisor had been filed to a point. Her beads and filed teeth indicate that she was born in Africa, and might have come from the Senegal-Gambia region of West Africa, where some people still file their teeth to indicate ethnic affiliation.

Now, in our century, this woman whose name we will never know,

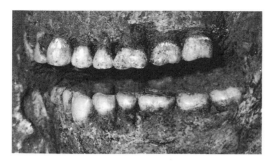

Several burials show evidence of modified teeth, a tradition among various African ethnic groups. *Dennis Seckler, photographer. Courtesy of General Services Administration.*

whose history no one wrote, this woman who may have been part of the cargo of a slave ship, her value calculated along with the price of rum, sugar, and firearms, this woman viewed by those who bought and sold her as a heathen African slave, would no longer be lost in time. She finally has a voice and can tell at least part of the story of Africans in early New York City.

Burial #340 was one of the most significant discoveries since the excavations had begun. A strand of about 111 waist beads lay around her hips. No burial had ever been found in North America with beads used in this way; however, waist beads have been worn in Africa for centuries. Some of the beads were cowrie shells, most of them were made of glass, and one bead was amber. Small blue and white beads also found near her remains had probably been wrapped around her wrists.

Beads were and still are important and powerful symbols in many West African cultures and in other cultures around the world. They have been used for exchange (as money) and to denote the important passages of life such as birth, marriage, and death. They were also used to keep the wearer from harm in life and to help the individual make the journey into the afterlife.[2]

Waist beads found *in situ* (in their original position when buried with the deceased) on Burial #340. *Dennis Seckler, photographer. Courtesy of General Services Administration.*

The number of valuable beads she was buried with (cowrie shells and amber) and the waist beads, which in certain African societies indicate the importance of the wearer, suggest that this woman may have been a respected person in the city's African community. She might have been the daughter of a king or a chief, kidnapped and caught up in the slave trade, or she might have had knowledge of remedies and healing.

Perhaps she had been honored by other blacks, both slave and free, because she was a direct link to their past. People like her could replenish memories of a fading African past and disappearing African traditions. Her presence may have been a constant reminder of what had been lost to slavery.

Burial #340 has a *terminus ante quem* date of 1740. Ceramics found in the shallow grave pit were manufactured between the years 1740 and 1796. The grave must have been extremely shallow because potters using this site as a dump dug almost into her coffin.

Analysis of the beads cannot tell the archaeologists exactly when the woman was buried, but chemical analysis can give some idea of when a bead was manufactured and when it was in use.

For example, one of the woman's beads was large and black, with wavy lines. The same kind of bead was used by the Iroquois people in New York State. These beads have been found in Iroquois sites dated 1682 to 1750, the same years that the African Burial Ground was in use.[3] Further research has to be undertaken to learn how Africans in New York during this period acquired their beads, and whether some beads were obtained from Native Americans.

The beads also give us an idea of where the woman might have come from. Though it is almost certain that she was born in Africa, she could have been brought to New York from Barbados.

New York slave traders often purchased Africans from slave markets

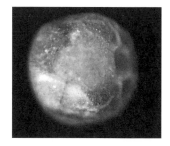

Most of Burial #340's beads were blue. Researchers note that in other burial sites in North America and South America where people of African descent are interred many blue beads have been found. Perhaps Burial #340 was buried in the African tradition where blue beads symbolize love for the deceased.[6]

in the Caribbean. One of the woman's beads is similar to beads found in the Newton Plantation site, a cemetery in Barbados where enslaved Africans and their descendants were buried from the late seventeenth to the early nineteenth century.[4] The Newton Plantation Cemetery existed during the same time period as the African Burial Ground in New York City. One of the burials in the Newton Cemetery contained cowrie shells, amber, and glass beads similar to those found in Burial #340. She could have been on one of the 113 vessels that brought in total of 672 slaves from Barbados between 1715 and 1764. (A total of 4,398 slaves entered New York in those years from other Caribbean islands and from South Carolina as well).[5]

Perhaps she had been on *The Eagle,* the ship that smuggled forty enslaved Africans from Guinea, West Africa, into Long Island, rather than coming through the port of New York. Slave smuggling was a thriving business, allowing traders and merchants to avoid paying taxes on their human property. The smuggled slaves would be brought into the city at a later date.

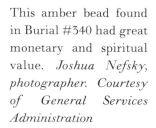

This amber bead found in Burial #340 had great monetary and spiritual value. *Joshua Nefsky, photographer. Courtesy of General Services Administration*

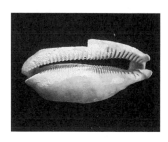

Cowrie shell found with the waist beads. *Joshua Nefsky, photographer. Courtesy of General Services Administration.*

Maybe she had been one of the 209 enslaved women, men, and children entering the Port of New York (today's South Street Seaport) on New York ships that had gone directly to Africa between 1701 and 1715.[7] (Of the slaves in the New York trade, 60 percent came from the Caribbean, and the remaining 40 percent came directly from Africa.)[8]

And if she'd come in on one of those ships after 1709, she stepped off the dock at Water Street and was marched, along with other enslaved people, to Wall Street, where she was auctioned off at the slave market there.[9]

Or, she might have been brought to New York on *The Catherine*, the slave ship that made two trips to Africa in the 1730s, bringing 260 enslaved Africans to New York and New Jersey.[10]

Of course, there is no way to tell what she experienced after her arrival, whom she was enslaved to, or what kind of work she was forced to do. Future analysis of her skeletal remains may show stress fractures, indicating certain types of labor.

What we do know is that she carried her African culture into captivity with her. She came, as did so many others, with religious and cultural traditions that did not die in the holds of slave ships, nor disappear in the houses of bondage. There is no way to know exactly the circumstances of this woman's death.

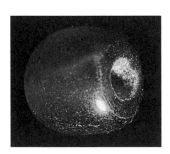

Blue glass bead. Blue beads were highly prized by many Africans as they were believed to ward off illness and evil. *Doville Nelson, photographer. Courtesy of General Services Administration.*

She may have died shortly after experiencing the terror of leaving Africa, the Middle Passage across the Atlantic, and arrival and enslavement in a strange place far from home. However, the people who buried her understood the meaning of her life and what it represented. She had been buried with care and respect.

Whoever laid her to rest had knowledge of some of the traditions that she brought with her. They may even have been from the same African ethnic group or a closely related group.

Alongside the world created in early New York by the Dutch and later by the English, there was a world created by the men and women of Africa and of African descent. Burial #340 probably always wore her beads under her skirts, apron, and other articles of European-style clothing. They were hidden, just as the cultural practices of Africans in colonial New York were hidden from the eyes of most whites.

As the slave trade increasingly became a source of labor and wealth for the colony, New York's leaders tried to control and rule the growing slave population with an iron hand. Enslaved men and women resisted, drawing strength and courage from that hidden African world.

CHAPTER 7

THE REVOLT OF 1712

The archaeologists began excavating Burial #25 on October 16, 1991. This burial was adjacent to two other graves in Republican Alley and was completely excavated by October 19. Though the coffin had eroded into the mottled yellow-brown soil, the skeletal remains were still intact. Coffin nails and ceramic fragments were also found in this grave.

Forensic specialists who examined the skeleton determined that the individual was an adult female. They were also able to determine how she died. A musket ball was lodged in her rib cage.

Why was she shot? Perhaps she'd tried to run away, as many enslaved New Yorkers attempted to do. However, runaway slaves would not be shot and killed—they were valuable property. A difficult person would be sold off so that the owner did not take a financial loss. If she had committed a crime under the colonial laws she would have been either hanged or burned at the stake. Perhaps she

Burial #25. Adult woman with lead bullet in her rib cage. *Dennis Seckler, photographer. Courtesy of General Services Administration.*

Visual analysis of the musket ball revealed that one side was flattened. Lead is a soft metal that deforms or flattens when it hits a body or object with force. This tells us that the ball was fired and the woman hit, presumably causing her death.

was shot during the attempted slave revolt of 1712.

We will never know why this woman was shot, but this burial reminds us of the brutality and instability of the lives of black people in the early years of the eighteenth century as slavery became the source of labor and wealth in the British American colony of New York. Like the remnants of African culture hidden and suppressed among the enslaved population, their anger and resentment often remained hidden as well.

Sometimes, however, the anger erupted. In 1708 a Native American man and a black woman—both slaves—killed the family who owned them. Colonial punishment was swift. The woman was burned at the stake and the man hanged.[1]

New York slave owners were frightened and outraged; however, they would be even more terrified when the rage of slaves exploded again in 1712.

On the night of April 6, Peter Van Tilburg's slave set fire to his master's outhouse, the signal for twenty-three other enslaved men to leave the fruit orchard on Maiden Lane. Armed with muskets, hatchets, swords, and knives they headed to the burning outhouse and waited. It wasn't long before a group of townspeople raced to the burning building.

Fire was a dangerous thing in colonial New York with its wooden homes, warehouses, and stores. An uncontrolled fire could easily spread through an entire block.

When the townspeople reached Van Tilburg's property, they had more than one kind of fire to contend with. The band of slaves began shooting at the crowd, killing nine and wounding five or six others. New York experienced its first slave revolt.

Fires were a common occurrence in colonial New York. *From Valentine,* Manual, *1860. Courtesy of New-York Historical Society.*

An artist's depiction of the harsh punishment carried out on enslaved Africans. *From Valentine,* Manual, *1860. Courtesy of New-York Historical Society.*

Governor Robert Hunter ordered soldiers from the fort to put down the rebellion, but the men had escaped into the woods beyond Maiden Lane. The militia scoured the woods and eventually captured seventeen rebels. Another six committed suicide rather than be captured.

All of the captured men were condemned and executed. As Governor Hunter reported to the authorities in Britain, "some were burnt, others hanged, one broke on the wheele and one hung alive in ye towne. There has been the most exemplary punishment inflicted that could be thought of."[2]

What made these men commit such a bold and desperate act? At their trial, some of the men stated that they revolted because they had been treated so cruelly and brutally by their masters. Some of them may have been free seamen on Spanish or French ships captured by the British, and some may have been among the 185 captive slaves brought into the city directly from Africa between the years 1710 and 1712.[3]

Life for blacks in New York had changed since the time of the Dutch colonists, when men like Simon Congo and Paolo d'Angola were able to petition the city council for a bit of freedom.

Restrictive laws kept slave owners from manumitting—or freeing—their slaves. Under a law passed in 1712, a slave owner had to have, as security, a large amount of money in order to provide a yearly income to the freed individual. This law effectively stopped owners from freeing their slaves. Slave owners complained, saying that their slaves would not serve them knowing that there was no chance of ever being freed.[4]

In other words, their slaves were not happy and content, and resisted their enslavement in any number of ways. Doing the minimal amount of work and performing it poorly was a form of resistance. Slaveholders sometimes would promise eventual freedom to a slave in order to ensure a man or woman's loyal service, because unless there was some chance of future liberty, resistance would continue. Setting fires, stealing, and running away to whomever happened to be enemies of the British, often the French and Spanish, were more outward forms of resistance. Escaped male slaves could get work as seamen on French and Spanish ships. Many fugitive slaves also escaped to nearby Native American settlements.

The General Assembly of the Province of New York passed a law in 1705 forbidding slaves from "travelling forty miles above the city of Albany, at or above a place called Sarachtoge [Saratoga], on pain of death."[5] (Under colonial laws, only the colony could execute a slave, not an individual owner. When the colony executed a slave, the owner was given a sum of money by the government to pay for his or her lost property.)

Sometimes slaves were freed, but with restrictions like those placed on the Africans freed by the Dutch in the 1600s. In 1708 the merchant Benjamin Faneuil freed Nero, his slave, but Nero was required to work for the family for ten years. Evidentally, Nero was a valuable laborer and Faneuil did not want to lose his services.

There were a few cases, too, where owners freed their slaves in their wills. In 1697 Mary Jansen Loockerman said that on her death, her slave Manuel would serve her daughter until he was twenty-five years old. Manuel was a child when the will was drawn. His parents agreed to the arrangement; probably they were also enslaved to Mary Loockerman.

The free black population continued to dwindle and was, with the exception of a few, barely distinguishable from enslaved blacks. One exception was Solomon Peters and his wife Maria Anthonis Portugues. Peters was a prosperous farmer who raised four sons and four daughters. "In his 1694 will Peters bequeathed his 'houses and lands and household goods' to his wife and left his four sons, 'all my iron tools and implements of husbandry, and all my guns, swords, pistols, and the like.' "[6] Possibly the Peters family was able to hold on to their farm in the Bowery because his will was drawn before the British crown passed a law in 1712 forbidding blacks, Indians or mulattoes (people of mixed race) from owning land. Under that law Peters's wife and children could not have inherited his land.

With no more danger of raids, and with the wilderness in the outlying region cleared by the black farmers and now "tamed," the town government wanted the land back. As the original black landowners died out, the new law effectively kept their children from inheriting the land. And unless their offspring had received manumission papers (certificates of freedom) they could possibly be re-enslaved as well.

New York street scene around 1700. *Photograph from Valentine,* Manual, *1858. Courtesy of New-York Historical Society.*

A number of the families stayed in the area working the same land and paying rent to the new white owners. This area of Manhattan remained an African-American section, known as Little Africa, until the middle of the 1800s.

By 1716, John Bastien's fifteen-acre property, the last piece of black-owned land, was sold. Today, the Empire State Building occupies some of that ground.

As additional enslaved people came into the colony, restrictions were placed on the movements of all blacks. Because of the incident of 1712, and fears of more slave revolts, the city ruled that only twelve black people could attend a burial and that funeral services could not be conducted at night. The iron shackles of slavery even reached the burial ground, the one place where the blacks had had a semblance of cultural freedom. However, they continued conducting night funerals in spite of the law.

As the number of restrictive laws and slave codes grew, the more enslaved people resisted. Also, there were not enough constables or sheriffs to control them.

In the decade after the 1712 revolt, a gallows was built on the common land near the burial ground, one of the first structures in the area. Until then, executions had taken place at the battery, on the southern end of the island. The Bridewell, the first prison, was erected

The Bridewell Prison. *From Valentine,* Manual, *1860. Courtesy of New-York Historical Society.*

there as well. Clearly, a message was being sent to Africans and people of African descent.

The shadow of the gallows didn't stop the resistance, though. It only seemed to make enslaved women and men more determined to fight against the dehumanizing slave system and the society that benefited from it.

CHAPTER 8

A CRUEL AND HARSH SEASON

Burial #340, the woman with the beads, was not the only burial that reflected African memories and cultural roots. Another burial, #101, also suggests an African past. The individual in this grave was a male, thirty to thirty-five years old. Two buttons made of bone and two brass pins were found with the remains, and tacks hammered into what appears to be the shape of a heart on the coffin lid hints at African images and symbols.

Was this actually a heart? Or was it something else? On close examination, the shape also had other, sketchy, unidentifiable forms within its outline. Some of the experts studying the remains and the artifacts began to think that the heart was one of many symbolic geometric forms called *adinkra* that are used by people in present-day Ghana and the Ivory Coast in West Africa—the region from which many people enslaved in the Caribbean and America were taken. The heart shape could be the symbol *Akoma*, meaning "have patience," a symbol of endurance.

Yet, perhaps, it is simply a heart, expressing love for the deceased by those he left behind. Whether it is a heart or an *adinkra* symbol, it shows us once again that Africans and people of African descent did not allow themselves to be brutalized by a society that saw them only as property.

By 1741 about one in every five persons in New York City was African or of

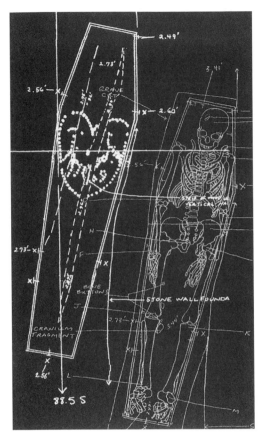

A possible *adinkra* symbol constructed out of metal tacks on the lid of the coffin of Burial #101. *Courtesy of New York Archeological Council.*

African descent. Out of a population of eleven thousand people, two thousand were black, and most of them were enslaved. About nine hundred individuals and families in the city held slaves, used primarily as domestic servants and artisans.[1] (In the counties such as Queens and Brooklyn and in the rest of the province, large numbers of slaves were employed as farm laborers.)

Who were these enslaved men, women, and children of New York City? How did they live and labor? Many of them were female and many were children under the age of sixteen. Most city slaveholders had one or two slaves used as domestic servants to do household work. Rich white families, however, would have as many as ten to twelve enslaved men, women, and children in their households. Some of them worked in the slaveholder's home, while others would work in the slaveholder's business or trade.

A letter written in 1721 by a prominent New Yorker, Cadwallader Colden, shows how young slaves were used in his household. He wrote to the agent who supplied slaves to buyers, "Please to buy mee two Negro men about eighteen years of age. I designe them for Labour & would have them strong & well made Please likewise to buy mee a Negro Girl of about thirteen years old my wife has told you that she designes her Cheifly to keep the children & to sow [sew] & theirfore would have her

Likely & one that appears to be good natured."[2] Cadwallader not only wanted a competent slave, but a happy slave as well.

Young men and women were preferred, especially as domestic servants. They performed such tasks as cleaning, cooking, making trips to the market for food, carrying drinking water from the "tea-water" pump (a water pump that gives potable water), washing, sewing, and on Sunday mornings carrying foot stoves containing live coals so that their master or mistress could have warm feet in church.

When slave traders brought their human cargo into the city to be sold, many of the advertisements spoke of the youth of the slaves. For example, one advertisement announced: "Parcel of likely Negro Boys and Girls, from 9 to 12 Years of age."[3]

The *New York Gazette* in 1730 advertised, for sale, "a Likely Negro Girl about 18 Years of Age, and a likely Negro Boy about 16 Years, both born in this City, they can speak good English and Dutch and are bred up to all sorts of House-work."[4]

The city's artisans depended on their skilled enslaved workers.

Wall Street slave market. This image appeared in a 1730 map of New York of the East River and Wall Street. *Courtesy of Eric Homberger.*

Potters, carpenters, blacksmiths, coopers (a person who makes and repairs barrels and casks), all employed enslaved men who helped their owners build profitable businesses. The blacksmith Harmanus Burger begged the city not to execute his slave, Harry, who had been accused of stealing. In his petition to the City Council, Burger described himself as a poor, lame, and elderly man. His only source of income was the labor his slave Harry performed.

If there was not enough work to keep a slave busy, owners often hired them out to someone else who might need them. The slave-holder would be paid for the work the slave performed. At times the city would hire slaves from individual owners to work on a public project, such as constructing a street.

Sometimes, though rarely, an owner would admit that most of his wealth was derived from the labor of a talented and faithful slave. A butcher, George Norton, freed one of his slaves, Sam, in his will. Sam had helped "to gain most part of his masters [sic] Wealth."[5]

For the richest New Yorkers, however, their adult male slaves were a status symbol. A black butler or coachman was just one more item of valuable property.

It was impossible, though, to turn human beings into docile chattel, especially in a city like New York, where a master or mistress could not watch a slave's every move. There were not enough constables and sheriffs to enforce the laws forbidding slaves to congregate, to go out without a pass, to frequent taverns and inns, and to associate with whites and free blacks. (In cases in 1715, 1716, and 1724 free blacks were fined for entertaining slaves.)[6] Wherever and whenever they could, the enslaved population defied the system. In 1741 the city's lawmakers, merchants, and other leaders tried to break that defiance.

It was a cruel and harsh season that began with a robbery committed on February 28, 1741.

Caesar and Prince walked quickly and silently along the deserted, narrow streets. They tried to merge into the midnight shadows as they headed toward the cluster of shops on Broad Street.

The two young men easily broke into one of the stores and stole silver candlesticks, money, and linen. They then hurriedly left the shop and rushed to John Hughson's tavern on Broadway, skillfully avoiding the constables and the citizen's night watch patrolling the streets.

As usual, John Hughson, the white tavern owner, took the stolen goods and paid Caesar. Prince went home, but Caesar relaxed for the rest of the evening at Hughson's tavern. He probably drank a few drams of rum, and maybe even ate a meal and socialized with other customers. In the morning, he left the tavern and returned to the bakery, where he fired up the furnace and began his day's work for his master, John Vaarck, a baker. Caesar was Vaarck's slave.

However, neither John Vaarck nor anyone else could master Caesar. He seized his own brand of freedom as he operated in the thriving criminal world of the city.

Stealing from the store and then selling the stolen merchandise wasn't the only crime Caesar had committed that February night. Going out without his master's permission, being out at night alone (except in an emergency), going to a tavern, were all crimes under New York's slave laws. If there were other enslaved men in the tavern, that would have been a crime as well, since enslaved people were not allowed to meet in groups of three or more unless they were working.

Caesar had a regular income from his "business" association with John Hughson, the tavern owner, and another white man, John Romme. Unlike Hughson, who was considered a low-class tavern owner, Romme was a respected gentleman because of his family connections. Romme purchased and sold any large items that Caesar stole.

John Vaarck, Caesar's master, had no complaints about Caesar's work. As long as Caesar performed his duties, Vaarck would let the sheriff deal with any laws that Caesar broke.

The burglary and transaction with Hughson went smoothly, and probably Caesar thought no more of it. It was all in a night's work. But on March 1, 1741, Caesar was arrested on suspicion of the February burglary. John Hughson was arrested as well, because the stolen property was found on his premises. He and his wife Sarah were released on bail.

Caesar remained in jail. He'd been jailed and publicly whipped in the past. The worst that could happen would be another public beating and his master could be fined for the troubles Caesar caused. Possibly, Caesar could be banished to one of the British colonies in the Caribbean.

John Hughson could be fined for allowing slaves to frequent his tavern and he, of course, would be punished for receiving stolen property.

This time, however, Caesar's and Hughson's fates were determined by forces and events that ensnared them and many others in a web of racism, prejudice, and hysteria. While Caesar sat in jail, and Hughson and his wife remained under a cloud of suspicion, the striking events of 1741 unfolded.

On March 18, the first fire broke out. At the southern tip of Manhattan, where the colony of New Amsterdam had been born over one hundred years earlier, Fort George was burning. Named after King George, the fort housed the royal governor, important papers and documents, and the guns and soldiers that protected the harbor and the city. Every man in the city who could get there rushed to the fort to help extinguish the fire and rescue the governor and the colony's records.

The March winds fanned the fire, so that even after hours of battling the blaze the fort, the governor's house, the chapel, the armory, the soldiers' barracks, and all of the other buildings that were part of the fort were engulfed in flames.

As the flames began to dance dangerously toward the homes of the rich residents on lower Broadway, panic set in. Strangers helped the lower Broadway residents remove clothing, furniture, and other valuables from their homes, which were in the line of fire. (Some of these good Samaritans also helped themselves to the valuables.) Fortunately, by nightfall it began to rain and the blaze was extinguished, but not before Fort George was entirely burned down. People were disturbed and commented on the destructive power of the fire that could have leveled the entire city. (In 1741 New York City only covered about five square miles of Manhattan island.)

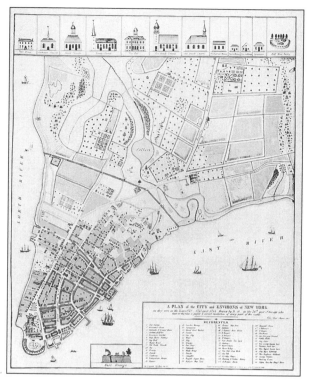

David Grim map. Image of New York landscape and city from 1742. *Courtesy of New-York Historical Society.*

On March 26 the alarms rang again—another fire near the torched fort. This time, though, the flames did not spread and the fire was soon quenched. Less than a week later, on April 1, fire blazed at Winant Van Zant's warehouse near the East River. The fire was contained before scorching other buildings.

Then, on April 4, flames leaped through a stable on Maiden Lane, but fast work by fire fighters kept the blaze from spreading beyond the roof and a haystack. Before the smoke cleared, another fire alarm rang out at a house near the stable. A straw mattress in a kitchen loft had been lit. Someone mentioned that a slave in that household slept in the kitchen loft.

On April 5, another fire, this time at attorney Joseph Murray's stables. Burning coals were found under a haystack. Memories of the 1712 slave revolt that began with a fire were revived. All of these fires couldn't be accidental, people said. That same Sunday, April 5, a woman named Abigail Earle overheard three black men make a comment about fires as they walked along Broadway. She informed the constable.

The tide of fear, hysteria, and racism began to rise on April 6, in the wake of four more fires. Many people believed that slaves were the cause and the roundup began, beginning with an enslaved man named Juan and four other Spanish blacks.

Someone had fingered Juan as a possible suspect because he always complained that he had been a free man until the Spanish vessel he and his shipmates worked on had been captured by a British ship in 1740.

Juan and his shipmates were taken to the City Hall for questioning. While these men were being questioned, another fire broke out in a warehouse near City Hall and a black man was seen running from the building.

In the midst of the fire, the running, and the confusion, someone shouted that the blacks were rising. Mobs of white men began to roam the streets, seizing black men and carrying them off to the City Hall jail.

Almost one hundred black men were rounded up and questioned on April 6, but the authorities learned nothing about the rash of fires. Angry citizens demanded that the councilmen get to the bottom of the growing rumors about a slave conspiracy to burn down the city and kill all whites. Every black male age sixteen and over became a dangerous enemy.

Young black men were the most valued of the enslaved population, yet they were the most feared and hated, especially when they were not servile.

A LIST OF NEGROES COMMITTED ON ACCOUNT OF THE CONSPIRACY.

NEGROES.	Masters or Owners	Committed	Arraigned	Convicted	Confessed.	Burnt.	Hanged.	Transported to	Discharged.
Antonio,	Peter De Lancey,	April 6,	June 13,	June 17.				Spanish W. Indies	
Augustine, } Spaniards.	Macmullen,	April 1,	June 13,	June 17.					
Antonio, }	Sarah Maynard,	April 1,	June 13,	June 17.				Madeira.	
Albany,	Mrs. Carpenter,	May 12,	June 8,	June 10.		June 12.			
Abraham, a free negro,		June 1,							
Adam,	J. Murray, esq.	June 26,			June 27.			Madeira.	
Brash,	Peter Jay,	May 9,	June 25,		June 25.			Madeira.	
Bastian alias Tom Peal,	Jacobus Vaarck,	May 12,	June 8,	June 10,	June 13,			Hispaniola.	
Ben,	Capt. Marshall,	June 9,	June 12,	June 13,			June 16.		
Bill alias Will,	C. Ten Eyck,	June 12,	July 3,		June 30,			Madeira.	
Bridgewater,	A. Van Horne,	June 22,	July 3,		June 27.			Hispaniola.	
Billy,	Mrs. Ellison,	June 25,	July 1,						
Braveboy,	Mrs. Kierstede,	June 27,	July 10,		June 30,			Madeira.	
Burlington,	Joseph Haines,	July 3,							July 15.
Cæsar,	Vaarck,	March 1,	April 24,	May 1,†			May 11,		
Cuffee,	A. Philipse, esq.	April 6,	May 28,	May 29,		May 30,			
Cuba, a wench,	Mrs. C. Lynch,	April 4,							5.
Curacoa Dick,	Cornelius Tiebout	May 9,	June 8,	June 10,		June 12,			
Cato,	Alderman Moore,	May 9,	July 15,		June 22,				
Cæsar,	do. Pintard,	May 9,	July 3,		June 22,			Madeira.	
Cuffee,	Lewis Gomez,	May 24,	June 6,	June 8,			June 9,		
Cæsar,	Benjamin Peck,	May 25,	June 6,	June 8,			June 9,		
Cato,	Joseph Cowley,	May 25,	June 12,	June 13,			June 16,		
Cook,	Gerardus Comfort	May 26,	June 6,	June 8,			9,		
Cambridge,	C. Codwise,	May 30,	July 10,		June 30,			Cape Francois.	
Cæsar,	Israel Horsefield,	May 30,	June 26,		June 27,			St. Thomas.	
Cato,	John Shurmur,	June 9,	June 16,	June 19,	June 27,		July 3,		

† Of a robbery, but appears to have been a principal negro conspirator.

The list on this and following four pages shows the names and sentences of some of the people who were accused of conspiring to burn down New York City. The accused were defined by their owers and the labor they perfomed. It is taken from the journal of the proceedings kept by Daniel Horsmanden, the prosecuting justice.

But the eighteenth-century city dwellers had a long list of people and ideas they hated and feared: strangers, foreigners, Spanish, Catholics, and the poor—white and black. Reports of slave rebellions in the Caribbean and in South Carolina (the Stono Rebellion of 1739, in which a force of about a hundred armed blacks in the region of the Stono River near Charleston, South Carolina, staged a rebellion, killing about a dozen whites) heightened fears and prejudices. Continuing wars with Spain added to those fears. New York's tradesmen and businessmen, shopkeepers, and slave traders wanted the city council to find and punish the arsonists and conspirators. Every new fire forged a greater conspiracy rumor—the slaves would burn down the city and the Spanish fleet would sail into New York's harbor and capture the colony. Whites were also implicated in the rumors.

Tongues began to wag and fingers point when the city council

NEGROES.	Masters or Owners	Committed	Arraigned	Convicted.	Confessed	Burnt.	Hanged.	Transported to	Discharged.
Caesar,	Corns. Kurtrecht,	June 9,	July 3,		July 2,			Hispaniola,	
Cato or Toby,	John Provoost,	9,	June 12,	June 13,			June 16,		
Cuffee,	Mrs. Fortune,	22,	July 15,		2,				
Cato,	Robert Benson,	23,	26,					Surinam.	
Cajoe alias Africa	Mordecai Gomez,	26,	1,		June 28,			Madeira.	
Caesar,	Alderman Moore,	29,							July 20.
Caesar,	Dr. Henderson,	29,	10,						15.
Cajoe,	Richard Baker,	30,							
Dundee,	Robert Todd,	May 7,	3,		24,			Cape Francois.	
Dick,	Robins,	July 8,							23.
Dublin,	Capt. Walton,	13,							23.
Deptford,	John Cruger, esq.	June 23,	June 26,		27,			Portugal.	
Dick,	C. Ten Eyck,	20,	July 15,		30,			Hispaniola.	
Dick,	Wolf,	23,	23,					Hispaniola.	
Diego,	Peter VanDursen,	27,							23.
Diego,	Marschalk,								23.
Emanuel, a Spaniard,	Thos. Wendover,	April 6,	June 25,		27,	June 12,		Hispaniola,	
Francis,	Jasper Bosch,	6,	8,	June 10,					
Fortune,	John Wilkins,	May 22,	July 7,		May 22,			Madeira,	
Fortune,	J. Vanderspiegle,	22,	June 12,	13,			June 16,		
Fortune,	John Latham,	June 13,	July 7,		June 15,			Curacoa.	
Fortune,	David Clarkson,	25,	1,		July 2,			Madeira.	
Frank,	F. Philipse, esq.	27,							20.
Fortune,	Capt. Walton,	28,	1,	July 15,			July 18,		
Frank,	Henry Ryker,	30,	10,	15,			18,		
Guy,	Tim. Horsefield,	May 30.	June 26,		June 27,			St. Thomas.	
Galloway,	H. Rutgers,	July 2,	July 10,	15,			18,		
Gosport or Jasper,	Robert Bound,	June 29,	1,	15,				Cape Francois.	

offered money to anyone who gave them information about a conspiracy. People accused of being part of the plan to capture the colony were offered leniency if they informed on others.

Daniel Horsmanden, the presiding justice, and the city council began their investigation on April 22, 1741. The judge vowed first to rid the city of all crime, beginning with people like John Hughson, who ran taverns and tippling houses where slaves were allowed to drink, dance, gamble, and enjoy a few hours of recreation. The city needed to enforce its slave laws. New York City's slaves had too much freedom and idle time, the judge declared.

Mary Burton, Hughson's indentured servant girl, was the first person to appear for questioning before the grand jury. Mary was told that if she spoke the truth she'd be freed from her indentured servitude. Freedom was a powerful lure. Mary's tongue and imagination loosened. She gave the jury an earful:

Caesar, Prince and Mr. Philipse's Negro man, Cuffee, used to meet frequently at my master's house, and I've heard them talk frequently of burning the fort and that they'd go down

A LIST OF NEGROES COMMITTED ON ACCOUNT OF THE CONSPIRACY.									
NEGROES.	Masters or Owners	Committed.	Arraigned.	Convicted.	Confessed.	Burnt.	Hanged.	Transported to	Discharged.
Harry,	Mrs. Kipp,	May 30	June 16	June 19	June 27		July 3		
Harry,	John Thurman,	June 9	19		22			Madeira	
Hanover,	John Cruger, jun.	29							July 15
Hereford,	Samuel M. Cohen,	29							2
Harry (Doctor)	J. Mizreal, L. I.	July 6	July 10	July 15		July 18			
Jack,	Joshua Slydall,	May 6	12		12			Cape Francois	
Jack,	Henry Breasted,	9	25		27			Hispaniola	
Jonneau,	Jacobus Vaarck,	13	7		July 2			Hispaniola	
Jamaica,	Thomas Ellison,	22	6	June 8				Madeira	
Jack,	Gerardus Comfort	26	June 6	8	June 8			Cape Francois	
Jeffery,	Capt. J. Brown,	June 15	July 1		27				
Jacob,	H. Rutgers,	23	June 26		24			Curacoa	
Jack,	J. Murray, esq.	25	July 1		26			Madeira	
John,	Widow Van Rantz,	27							July 20
Jack,	Jacob Abrahamse,	28	1		July 2				
Jack,	John Roerback,	28							20
Jack,	Judah Hayes,	July 2							6
John,	Rip Van Dam, esq.	6							20
Jupiter,	Capt. Walton,	13						Madeira	.
Kid,	C. Van Horne,	June 29							2
London,	Augustine Hicks,	May 30							June 4
London,	Peter Marschalk,	June 9	June 16	June 19	June 20			Madeira	
London,	Edward Kelly,	12	19		July 2			Hispaniola	
Lowe,	David Provoost,	22	25		June 27			Statia	
London,	Ben. Wyncoop,	22	26		25			Hispaniola	
London,	Roger French,	22	July 3		24			Madeira	
Lewis,	Adoniah Schuyler,	27	1		July 1			Madeira	
Mars,	Robert Benson,	12	3		3				

to the Fly and burn the whole town. My master and mistress said they'd aid and assist them as much as they could. In their common conversations they used to say that when all this was done, Caesar'd be governor and Hughson, my master, should be king.[7]

Burton's testimony ultimately unleashed a reign of terror. Judge Horsmanden and the city council attempted to stamp out crime, criminals, rebellious slaves, Catholics, spies, and anyone else who would destroy the colony.

On Friday, May 1, Caesar and Prince were tried before a jury of twelve men, on felony charges. They denied the charges; however, the jury found them guilty. On the following Friday, May 8, Justice Horsmanden delivered the sentence:

I have great reason to believe, that the crimes you now stand convicted of, are not the least of those you have been concerned in; for by your general characters you have been very wicked fellows, hardened sinners, and ripe, as well as ready,

A LIST OF NEGROES COMMITTED ON ACCOUNT OF THE CONSPIRACY.

NEGROES.	Masters or Owners.	Committed.	Arraigned.	Convicted.	Confessed.	Burnt.	Hanged	Transported to	Discharged.
Mink,	John Groesbeck,	June 12	June 16		June 18			Newfoundland	
Othello,	J. De Lancey, esq.	27	July 10	July 10	30		July 18		
Prince, [iard,	John Auboyneau,	March 2	April 24	May 1*			May 11		
Pablo or Powlus a Span-	Frederick Becker,	April 6	June 13	June 17				Newfoundland	
Patrick,	William English,	May 9	25		27			Madeira	
Prince,	Anthony Duane,	June 1	25	26			July 3		
Pompey,	Abraham Lefferts,	1	July 3		9			Madeira	
Primus,	James Debrosses,	12	3		19			St. Thomas	
Pedro,	Peter De Peyster,	13			29				
Prince,	Gabriel Crooke,	13	15		13				July 20
Pompey,	Peter De Lancey,	20	15		22			Cape Francois	
Pompey,	Jane Gilbert,	23	June 26		27			Madeira	
Pompey,	Samuel Bayard,	23	26		30			Madeira	
Phæton,	Nicholas Bayard,	30							15
Prince,	Corns. Kortrecht,	July 1	July 23				18	Hispaniola	
Quack,	John Walters,	April 6	10	July 10			18		
Quack,	John Roosevelt,	May 12	May 28	May 29	at the stake	May30			
Quamino,	Eben. Pemberton,	June 12	June 19		June 22			Madeira	
Quack,	Jacob Goelet,	July 4							23
Quash,	H. Rutgers,	June 9	12	June 13		June16			
Quash,	Le Roux,	July 2	July 23					Madeira	6
Robin,	John Chambers,	April 13	June 6	8		ς			
Robin,	Mrs. Bickley,	July 1							20
Sarah,	De Peyster,	April 4							11
Sarah,	Thomas Niblet,	May 10							
Sandy,	Thomas Niblet,	14						Hispaniola	
Sarah	Mrs. Burk,	25	July 7		1			Hispaniola	

Of a robbery, but appears to have been a principal negro conspirator.

for the most enormous and daring enterprizes, especially you, Caesar . . . you Caesar and you Prince, are to be taken hence to the place of execution, and there you, and each of you, are to be hanged by the neck until you be dead. . . .[8]

Caesar and Prince were hanged in the Commons near the burial ground. After his execution, Caesar's corpse was chained and hanged on the gibbet (platform) placed on the small island where the city's powderhouse stood. His body was left to rot and hang for over eleven weeks—a message to other slaves who would dare take liberties.

By July almost every black male aged sixteen and over was in jail, as the conspiracy investigations continued.

From May 11 to August 29, thirty black men were executed at the city commons; thirteen were burned at the stake, and seventeen were hanged. Two white women and two white men were executed as well.

Sarah Hughson, the tavern owner's wife, and Peggy, an Irish woman who associated with Caesar and lived with the Hughsons, were hanged. Mary Burton's testimony helped put the hangman's noose around their necks. John Hughson, the tavern owner, and John Ury, an

A LIST OF NEGROES COMMITTED ON ACCOUNT OF THE CONSPIRACY.

NEGROES.	Masters or Owners.	Committed.	Arraigned.	Convicted.	Confessed.	Burnt.	Hanged.	Transported to	Discharged.
Sam,	George Rappelie,	May 30							June 4
Scipio,	Mrs. Van Borsom,	June 9	June 25		June 25				
Sterling,	Capt. Lawrence,	12	July 3		23			Hispaniola	
Sam,	Peter Lowe,	22	June 26		July 3				
Scipio,	Robert Bound,	22	26		2			Cape Francois	
Sam,	Frederick Courtlandt,	23	26		1			Madeira	
Scipio,	Abraham Abrahamse,	25	26		June 27				
Scotland,	Nathaniel Marston,	27	July 7		29			Curacoa	
Sussex,	Mrs. Beekly,	July 1							July 29
Tickle alias Will,	Mrs. Carpenter,	May 30			12			Hispaniola	
Tom,	Winant Van Zandt,	30							2
Tom,	Benjamin Moore,	June 1	June 16		18			Newfoundland	
Tom,	Capt. Rowe,	12	July 3		July 2				
Tom,	Van Zant,	29							2
Toney,	John Latham,	13	June 25	June 26			July 3		
Toney,	Mrs. Brazier,	22	26		2			Surinam	
Tom,	Simeon Soumaien,	23	26		June 26				
Toby,	Widow Brestead,	25	July 1		30			Cape Francois	
Tom,	Hyer,	26	1	July 15				Hispaniola	
Tom,	Robert Livingston,	26			27			Madeira	
Titus,	Capt. Phœnix,	27	7		30			Surinam	
Tony or Tonio,	Counsellor Courtlandt,	29							28
Tom,	Peter Valette,	30							23
Toby,	Hercules Wendover,	30	10	15					
Toby,	Abraham Marschalk,	30							
Tom,	Bradt,	Feb. 15		March 2, 1742			Mar. 13, 1742		
Venture,	Cornelius Tiebout,	June 28	1	July 15			July 18, 1741		
Wan or Juan,	Capt. Sarly,	April 6	June 13	June 17			August 15		

A LIST OF NEGROES COMMITTED ON ACCOUNT OF THE CONSPIRACY.

NEGROES.	Masters or Owners.	Committed.	Arraigned.	Convicted.	Confessed.	Burnt.	Hanged.	Transported to	Discharged.
Will, a Spaniard	Abraham Filkins,	April 6							July 20
Wan,	Dr. Nicoll,	24							June 30
Will alias Gill,	Capt. Lush,	May 24	June 25		June 27			Hispaniola	
Worcester,	Isaac Varyan,	30	19		22			Cape Francois	
Will,	Anthony Ward,	June 20	25		at the stake	July 4			
Will,	Jacobus Vaarck,	20	25						
Windsor,	Samuel Myers Cohen,	25	July 1		June 30				
Warwick,	Obadiah Hunt,	25	1		July 1			Madeira	
Will,	John Tiebout,	July 4							July 23
Wan, Indian,	Lowe,	June 12	June 19		June 19			Curacoa	
York,	Benjamin Peck,	May 30	25		27			Madeira	
York,	Peter Marschalk,	June 9	16	June 19	20		July 3*		
York,	Thomas Thomase,	20	July 6		27			Madeira	
York,	Charles Crooke,	22	June 26		27				
York,	Widow Van Rantz,	July 1	July 23					Curacoa	
York,	Gerardus Dyckink,	2							13

* In chains with John Hughson.

NEGROES INDICTED WHO WERE NOT TO BE FOUND.

Hanover,	H. Cruger's.
London,	A. Van Horne's
Ben,	Stephen Bayard's.
Pedro,	R. Stillwell's.
Ben,	Augustus Jay's.
Jack,	Governeur's.
Joe,	Holt's.

Englishman suspected of being a Catholic priest and a spy, were hanged as well.

Hughson's body was also left to rot in public, along with Caesar's corpse—another grisly message sent to any New Yorkers who had criminal urges and dared defy the laws of the city council.

Of the other approximately one hundred black men arrested, seventy-two were banished from the Colony and sent into slavery elsewhere: the Caribbean, Portugal, Madeira, or Newfoundland. Thirty-three others were sent back to their owners.

The rumors of a slave conspiracy in 1741 generated the same kind of hysteria as the Salem Witch Trials fifty years earlier. Was there really a conspiracy? Possibly, but probably not as far-reaching as the rumors claimed.

Several enslaved men confessed to setting fires, either as revenge against a slave owner or as a way to steal property. One of the men executed admitted to burning down the fort. His wife was the governor's cook and he had been refused admittance to the fort to visit her.

The physical anthropologists think that they may have identified two burials showing signs of burning. When there is vertical cracking along the bone with evidence of white and black blotching and the bone becomes like chalk, it is called calcine bone and suggests that the individual was burned to death.

Caesar's body was brought down from the platform and placed, most likely, in the African Burial Ground. Prince and the other blacks who were hanged were probably interred there as well. Those closest to Caesar went to the gallows with him, so there was probably no one to mourn him.

Perhaps at night, in that far and remote place, where the hills descended into the ravine, someone may have wailed the cries for the dead and prayed for all of those executed during that cruel and harsh season.

CHAPTER 9

AFTERMATH

The gallows and the African Burial Ground at the edge of the city were, for many New Yorkers, sad and shameful reminders of the events of 1741. David Grim, writing his memoirs seventy-two years after the trials said,

> I have a perfect idea [memory] of seeing the [N]egroes chained to a stake and there burned to death.
>
> The place of this execution was in the valley between Windmill Hill and Pot-baker's Hill. . . . The public executions were continued here for many years afterwards. . . .
>
> Caesar a black man, a principal of the [N]egroes in this plot, was also hanged in chains, on a gibbet, at the south-east corner of the old Powder House, in Magazine Street [now Pearl Street].[1]

New Yorkers who experienced the episode firsthand, also had a perfect idea of the endless trials, burnings, hangings, and the sight and smell of corpses rotting for weeks. Many of them wanted to forget and resume their daily work, putting that terrible past behind them.

Other New Yorkers began to question the fairness of the trials and the severity of the sentences. Some people even began to ridicule the whole idea of a plot, and slaveholders tried to get compensation from the province for the loss of their slaves who had been executed.

However, black New Yorkers—both slave and free—could not forget, and would view the trials as just one more indication of their vulnerability in a society that refused to recognize their humanity.

The Commons, where Caesar and the others hanged and burned, was near the burial ground and near the land that used to belong to Catelina Anthony and the other Africans who owned farms on the "Negro frontier," or "Negro coast," as the area was called. A number of the descendants of those original black settlers still lived there.

As they went about their daily business they lived with the constant reminders of those terror-filled days: The gallows on the Commons, the crowds of people witnessing the executions, and the screams of the condemned men as the fire consumed them, became a permanent part of their world—an indelible memory.

A number of black New Yorkers were probably connected in some way to those men who were executed and those who were banished.

Most likely there were few black adults who did not know at least one of the accused in the 1741 conspiracy trials, or someone who knew one of those charged. Probably some of the condemned men left women and children behind to mourn them.

What would a new year bring to the city? Would there be more stability and less crime? Would slaves and indentured servants and poor people in general behave themselves and obey the laws? Would they no longer resist slavery and oppression?

On January 2, 1742, George Clarke, governor of the province of New York, wrote to the mayor and other city officials reminding them of the events of 1741. He warned that "the insolence of the [N]egroes is as great, if not greater than ever, and they are not only suffered to have private but even public meetings in great numbers. . . ." The governor charged the officials to make sure that the "laws against

[N]egroes" are obeyed. He warned the mayor and other city officials to keep watchful eyes on blacks, making certain that the laws forbidding slaves to meet in public or in private were strictly enforced. He also said that the conspiracy was "the hellish and barbarous designs of a blood-thirsty people, for the ruin and destruction of the whole province and the inhabitants thereof."[2]

The governor's letter was an echo from the previous year. Evidently, resistance to slavery and to oppressive laws had not been stamped out by the hangman's noose or the threat of a fiery death.

On Tuesday, February 2, 1742, at the quarterly meeting of the city's judges and officials, Judge Horsmanden read the governor's letter. The judge, underscoring the governor's warning, recommended that the grand jury investigate tavern keepers who allowed slaves to socialize in their establishments.

"A crime of the worst sort, a vile practice," he declared. Horsmanden wanted his colleagues to be as anxious as he was to punish all violators of the slave code. Horsmanden and Clarke both believed that there were still dangerous people in the city who had been involved in the 1741 conspiracy. He warned his colleagues and friends against feeling too secure.

Two weeks after this meeting, Horsmanden thought he'd found the proof he needed to mount a thorough conspiracy investigation and continue to root out enemies of the colony.

On Monday, February 15, at six in the morning, a carpenter, about to begin his work, discovered burning coals in the gutter of a shed near the old Dutch churchyard on Broad Street. The carpenter woke the owner of the building and the two men extinguished the blaze.

The men thought that the fire seemed suspicious and informed Mayor John Cruger. The mayor called a meeting of the city's magistrates that very morning.

The mayor and the magistrates hurried to the scene to investigate.

They inquired whether any slaves lived in the neighborhood and whether any of them were untrustworthy and suspicious characters.

The first person they found was Tom, the slave of a widow, Divertie Bradt, who owned a bakery near the church yard.

Tom was about twenty-one or twenty-two years old and was described as a simple half-witted fellow. Horsmanden said that Tom's face was not pleasant and that he looked guilty. Not only did his face indicate guilt in the minds of the investigators, but his occupation made him suspect as well. Bakery workers dealt with fire, and were up very early to get the ovens started for the day's baking. It appeared to the investigators that Tom could easily have thrown hot coals into the gutter from the baker's yard.

A heavy cloud of suspicion began to form over poor Tom's head. He, along with three other black men, were brought before the court for further questioning that morning.

The three men were eventually discharged, but Tom remained in custody. At three o'clock that afternoon, he was questioned before the magistrates and confessed that a week ago on Sunday he'd been talking to two young men, and one of them told him to set fire to his mistress's bakery, so that the fire could spread to other homes in the city. Blacks in the city, along with blacks coming in from Long Island, would kill all of the whites. Tom claimed that one of the men threatened to poison him if he didn't start a fire.

Tom was brought before the justices three more times—on February 16, 18, and 25. On February 25, Divertie Bradt was allowed by the court to question him. He changed his story, and said that no one told him to throw the coal and he didn't know why he threw it. He said that his owner, the widow Bradt, treated him well and he was not angry with her.

The investigators also found out that one of the men Tom named was nine miles out of the city on the Sunday he was supposed to have told Tom to burn down Bradt's house.

The other men Tom implicated were questioned again and denied knowing anything about a plot to burn down the city. Because he had lied about one of the men, Tom's confession could not be used to convict the others.

On Tuesday, March 2, Tom went before the justices. (Had his owner been willing to pay a small fee he could have had a jury trial.) He was found guilty of conspiring with others "to burn the whole town and city of New York." Tom denied this, and only confessed to starting a fire. However, before he was about to be hanged, he once again said that some men he knew told him to start the fire.[3]

It seemed as though the events of 1741 would be repeated in 1742. Tom was hanged on Saturday, March 13. The men he named were questioned once again; however, unlike the people who "confessed" to crimes in 1741, hoping to free themselves, these men insisted that they knew of no plot to burn down the city and had not told Tom to burn widow Bradt's house. They were released. On Monday, March 15, a fire was discovered on a tanner's premises, located on the east side of Manhattan in an area called Beekman Swamp. The tanner's slave, Sam, put out the fire; however, the fire had spread and so had suspicions.

Once again, there was a round of questions and investigations. On March 23, when someone threw a fiery bundle of linen into the gutter near a brew house, the owner's servants were questioned, but no one was accused of starting the fire.

On Tuesday, April 20, a grand jury was charged with discovering more about the fire at the tannery and the tanner's slave, Sam. But here, too, nothing was found and the matter was dropped. Evidentally, the city officials had no stomach for repeating the events of 1741.

The only justice dispensed this time was fines to nine tavern owners who ran what the keepers of the peace called "disorderly houses."

Justice Horsmanden had to content himself with ending the August
3 general quarter sessions of the peace with a warning to the officials
to strictly enforce the laws and rid the city of all "the mean ale-houses
and tippling houses . . . and to make out all such to this court, who
make it a practice . . . of entertaining [N]egroes, and the scum and
dregs of white people. . . . In general, you are charged to present all
crimes and offences which shall come to your knowledge, from trea-
sons, down to trespasses."[4]

The lives of the enslaved people of New York had reached their
lowest point.[5] However, slowly and subtly, the nature of slavery in the
city began to change, and this change might have been a direct result
of the 1741 episode.

For example, fewer enslaved men and women were imported from
the Caribbean after 1741. Also, fewer slaves came into the colony after
that year.[6]

The number of adult male slaves in the city dropped slightly. Many
were sent to Staten Island to labor on farms there. There seemed to be
a preference for young slaves, especially after the events of 1741. "For
this market they must be young, the younger the better if not quite
Children," a New Yorker wrote in 1762.[7] Children were easier than
adults to train and control.

Even though the system of slavery may have been slowly changing
in the city, the lives of enslaved men, women, and children were still
severe. Analysis of the skeletal remains in the burial ground reveals
just how difficult their lives were.

CHAPTER 10

RECOVERING THE PAST

While the archaeologists in New York continue to process and study the artifacts from the burial ground, physical anthropologists at Howard University in Washington, D.C., are analyzing the skeletal remains. Both groups of scientists will eventually be able to show in greater detail what life was like for the thousands of African men, women, and children and those of African descent who lived in colonial New York. To do this, the physical anthropologists use theories and methods of a field of study called taphonomy.

Forensic anthropology and the study of taphonomy are ways of studying the dead and their manner of burial in order to determine the cause of their death. Scientists analyze how the bones deteriorated and how quickly the body decomposed. Different diseases will leave bones in different states of preservation. Some diseases, such as yaws (an infectious tropical disease), will leave scarred bone that looks like tree bark. Tuberculosis will also leave scarring—the interior of the rib cage will be scarred and the spine will be deformed. Diseases such as arthritis, rickets, and anemia (all of which were found in the burial ground population), can be identified by the condition of the bones.

Scientists also conduct DNA tests in order to determine the ethnicity of an

Processing Skeletal Remains

a. After the remains were brought to the Howard University Laboratory they were carefully cleaned.

b. Dirt was brought from grave surfaces so that the scientists could sift through the soil to take out seed and plant material and small artifacts, such as shroud pins. Some bones were so fragile they were excavated with a large amount of dirt surrounding them for support. This method of excavation is called pedestalling.

c. The anthropologists slowly picked away at the remaining dirt.

d. Bone fragments were reconstructed to rejoin broken sections. If the skull was collapsed, it was also reconstructed.

e. Anthropometric measurements of the pelvis, skull, and other areas were taken in order to determine sex, race, age, etc.

f. The Howard University scientists also conducted a pilot study of DNA from some of the long bones (legs and arms).

Archaeologist painstakingly excavating fragile remains. *Dennis Seckler, photographer. Courtesy of General Services Administration.*

individual and to find out whether the individual had a genetic disease such as sickle-cell anemia.

Out of what is believed to be possibly ten thousand burials, four hundred have been excavated for study. Two hundred of these are burials of children, many under two years of age, indicating a high infant mortality rate. Then, as now, children cannot prosper and grow when the adults who care for them are not thriving.

In May of 1992, the archaeologists made a touching discovery: the remains of a mother buried with her infant nestled in the crook of her arm. Most likely, she had died giving birth to her child. Childbirth was dangerous for all women. It was particularly dangerous for women who had only the minimum of care and comfort.

Was she in a weakened condition from overwork? Did she sleep, for instance, in a damp basement or a cold kitchen? Were she and her baby victims of one of the cholera or smallpox epidemics that periodically swept the city? (Polluted water and other sanitary problems affected all New Yorkers, making them vul-

Burial of mother and child. *Dennis Seckler, photographer. Courtesy of General Services Administration.*

nerable to infectious diseases. In 1702 and again in 1731, smallpox and yellow fever epidemics ravaged the city's population.)

Through analysis of the skeletal remains, scientists are learning more about the burial ground population. What kind of health problems did children and adults have? What types of food did they eat? How did their work affect them physically?

Colonial life was grim for anyone who was poor. As the anthropological findings from the burial ground indicate, it was especially bitter for the black population.

The life of enslaved individuals of the eighteenth century was physically debilitating. Many of the skeletal remains from the African Burial Ground show signs of deep trauma to the bone, such as lipping on the spine. This is a condition where the vertebrae of the spine start to grow additional bone along the edges and start to lip or curl, even-

This is an image of *lipping*, in which the vertebra edge grows and curls over, causing deformity of the spine. Lipping normally afflicts the elderly and people with advanced spinal arthritis. However, among the burial ground population young men and women were afflicted as well, due to intense backbreaking labor. *Dennis Seckler, photographer. Courtesy of General Services Administration.*

tually causing severely painful arthritis. Damage to other joints such as knees, neck, and elbows, which can be evidence of arthritis, was also found. These conditions were discovered on relatively young adults. On other skeletal remains, there were fractures on the base of the skull and spine that could have been caused by carrying cargo and heavy loads on the head, which in some cases was probably the cause of death.

Children also may have been used to carry large, heavy loads and to do long repetitive jobs. These children did not have a childhood as we know it today; they were treated as just smaller adults and used for tasks that far exceeded their physical abilities. The physical anthropologists have found evidence of tearing of the muscles from the bone and lesions on the surfaces of the bone, which would be caused by heavy labor.

Analysis of teeth and bones of many of the burials of children indicate poor nutrition and a limited diet, high in sugar and other carbohydrates such as corn and flour. For example, a nine-year-old child had cavities on baby teeth and permanent teeth.[1]

In another burial, a five-year-old child's health problems were evident in tooth enamel that failed to form as the child's teeth developed.

The skeletal remains of children also indicate health problems caused by the mother's poor nutrition. Abnormal tooth enamel in the remains of one four-year-old could be the result of lack of milk. In those days all women breast-fed their babies. If a mother was ill and could not breast-feed her child, the infant would not be properly nourished.

Analyses of the remains of the child who wore the earbob (see photograph on page 13) indicate that she was very young and very sickly.

Some of the children had delayed development of their bones, as well as rickets (soft and deformed bones) from lack of calcium and vitamin D and inadequate sunlight. Children of enslaved mothers may have spent an unusual amount of time in dark kitchens or basements where their mothers had to work.

The Howard anthropologists also observed a high rate of birth defects, such as cleft palate (a split in the roof of the mouth) and delayed brain development. The scientists say that finding eleven children who have these birth defects (craniosynostosis, premature closing of the skull bones) "is an abnormally high rate of pathology; such conditions naturally occur in about one out of every 5,000 children today."[2]

The adult remains also show a life of hard work and few comforts. Scientists report that most of these individuals also had dental problems. For example, the woman with the musket ball in her rib cage had lost teeth to cavities.

Many of the adult skeletons show neck fractures from carrying heavy loads on their heads and fractures of the lower and lower middle back. Some fractures were probably caused by years of grueling labor, such as building houses, digging, shoveling, and farmwork.[3]

The work of the anthropologists and archaeologists continues. In the future they will be able to analyze food deposits (calculus) on the adult teeth and be able to tell more about the kind of diet people had. The scientists will also be able to give more information about the causes of death as well as the ways of life of the black population of colonial New York.

The burial ground in the years to come would be used not only to inter people of African descent but would also be the final resting place of victims of the war that would forever change the British-American colonies.

When the tides of war and revolution washed over the colonial shores thoughts of freedom from British rule began to fill the hearts and minds of the colonists. However, the people held in slavery had been rehearsing for their day of liberation for over a century.

CHAPTER 11

A BRAVE AND GALLANT SOLDIER

Thirteen years after the horrors of the conspiracy trials of 1741, instability loomed once again on the New York horizon, this time, in the form of war. For a few black men, however, this war would be the beginning of a long journey to freedom and equality.

The journey began on July 3, 1754, in the Ohio River valley. As French colonists tightened their control of this area, fighting broke out in Pennsylvania. A twenty-two-year-old colonel, George Washington, attacked a French outpost and lost a daylong battle.

By 1755, still losing battles and suffering chronic manpower shortages, the colonists also lost some of their apprehensions about putting guns in black hands and enlisted men of African descent into local militias. Colonial militias excluded blacks except in an emergency. The muster rolls for New York give us an idea of the rich mixture of people of African descent who lived and worked in colonial New York.

New York wasn't the only colony making use of its black population. North Carolina, Connecticut, Rhode Island, and Massachusetts all had a few blacks in their militias. For an enslaved man, serving in the militia was often a way to gain freedom. Free blacks who joined militias sometimes found relief from their difficult lives through increased wages and steady employment after serving.

The following is a list of black troops who served during the French and Indian War. These were among the earliest black troops serving in the American colonies.

MUSTER ROLLS OF NEW YORK PROVINCIAL TROOPS 1758

Muster Roll of A Company of Province in the Day of the province of New York as part of ye Quote of Queens County commanded by Petrus Stuyvesant 1758

Petrus Stuyvesant Captain
David Jones, Morris Smith, Lieutenants
Simeon Smith, George Dunbar, James Man, Cornelius Turner, Seargeants
Jeremiah Finch, John Walter, Mathew Robinson, Corporals

A Age and Size Roll of the Detachment of New York Troops Commanded by Captain John McEvers May 1st, 1758

Privates	Height	Age	Where Born	Trade	Complection	When Enlisted
Simeon Smith	5′ 9″	28	Jamaica	Shoemaker	Dark	April 1
Pomp Messenger	5′ 4″	20	Jamaica		Black	April 5
Coleman Ludlum	—	—	Jamaica		Negro	April 21

Men's Name	Age	Trade	Size	Where Born	Eyes	Hair	Visage	Complection
#49 - Philip Quick	18	—	5′8″	East Jersey	—	—	—	Negro
#56 - Henry Dean	28	—	5′10″	New York	—	—	—	Mulatta

A Muster Roll of the Men Raised and Passed Muster for the City and County of New York For Captain Abraham DeForrest's Company May 8th, 1760

Constant O'Brian Lieutenant, Nicholas Beckels Lieutenent

#31 - John Johnson	21	Cooper	5′5″	Nevis	—	—	—	Negro

A Muster Roll of the Men Raised and Passed Muster for the City and County of New York for Captain Barnaby Byrn's Co. New York March the 24th 1760

Men's Name	Age	Trade	Size	Where Born	Eyes	Hair	Visage	Complection
William Rannels	22	Labourer	5′11″	Ireland	—	—	—	Brown Mulato
James Sands	19	Tanner	5′7.5″	American	—	—	—	Negro
Paul Hall	19	Labourer	6′.5″	American	—	—	—	Negro

A MUSTER ROLL OF THE MEN RAISED AND PASSED FOR THE CITY OF NEW YORK FOR CAPTAIN HUBBELL'S CO. APRIL 1760

Men's Name	Age	Trade	Size	Where Born	Eyes	Hair	Visage	Complection
Francisco Coslea	23	Labourer	5′10″	Spain	—	—	—	Dark Mulatto
Daniel Penny	23	Labourer	5′8″	Block Island	—	—	—	Black Indian
Peter Calumpoe	30	Mariner	6′0″	Spain	—	—	—	Negro
Theodo Twawoolshead	25	Mariner	5′5″	Spain	—	—	—	Negro

A Muster Roll of the Men Raised and Passed Muster for the City of New York for Captain _____ Company 17th April 1762 embarked same day

    [Patrick Welsh]
    Ambrose Horton Lieutenants

Men's Name	Age	Born	Trade	Stature
John Dego, Negro	29	Portangale	Mariner	5′6″

By 1763, the American colonies won the French and Indian War with the help of troops from Britain; however, the relationship between the American colonies and Britain would drastically change when the British Parliament levied the first of many taxes to pay for the cost of the war.

The separate colonies had already begun to think collectively

> Many of the coins found on the eyelids of the deceased were minted during the reigns of King George II (1727–60) and King George III (1760–1820). Both kings ruled during a period that witnessed the French and Indian War and the War for Independence.

as they fought a common enemy. Murmurings of discontent began to be heard from New Hampshire to Georgia. The colonists protested against oppressive taxes and unfair laws. They accused Britain of tyranny, and of turning them into vassals and slaves.

Cries of liberty, freedom, and equality were on the lips of many. And those cries did not fall on white ears only. Blacks and other people of color heard them, too.

For some blacks in New York during these tumultuous years, the growing rift between England and her American colonies sparked hopes for their own struggles for liberty and independence. Some of them sincerely believed in the patriots' cause.

For example, Samuel Fraunces, probably a free man of color from one of the Caribbean islands, was a popular innkeeper and caterer. In

British copper coin. Coins such as this were often placed on the eyes of the deceased as a grave tribute as well as to keep the eyelids closed. Five coins were discovered at various grave sites. Three of them were recovered from eye sockets. *Dennis Seckler, photographer. Courtesy of General Services Administration.*

1762 he opened an inn on Broad and Pearl streets. Fraunces Tavern was a regular meeting place for disgruntled merchants and tradesmen. About 1765 they organized the Sons of Liberty to protest the Stamp Act, a tax on all printed materials. The organization spread from New York to other cities.

Fraunces Tavern, at Broad and Pearl streets, New York. *From Valentine*, Manual, *1854.*

Five years later in Boston, Crispus Attucks, a man of African and Native American descent, was among the crowds of workers protesting taxation when British troops opened fire in the episode known as the Boston Massacre.

By 1774, the American patriots wanted more than reform and repeal of unfair laws. They wanted their independence. The enslaved and partly free blacks who lived among them wanted their independence also. The American Revolution would become their fight for freedom, too.

When a force of about three hundred British soldiers entered the town of Lexington, Massachusetts, in the dawn of April 19, 1775, a black man, Prince Estabrook, was among the small force of American militiamen gathered on the town common to meet the redcoats. Prince Estabrook wasn't the only man of African descent defending the town that fateful day.

Peter Salem was there, too. His owner had freed him so that Salem could join the militia. There were other black men at Lexington and Concord and Bunker Hill: Pompy, Cato Stedman, Cato Bordman, Cuff Whittemore, Cato Wood, Pomp Blackman, and Barzillai Lew, a veteran of the French and Indian War.[1]

Back in New York, Samuel Fraunces let his wife run the tavern when he joined George Washington's division. By June, however, military and civilian leaders, trying to create an army out of small local militias, began to have second thoughts about enlisting blacks and Native Americans. Some enslaved men were freeing themselves by joining the militias, and the army did not want to enlist fugitive slaves.

Georgia and South Carolina, with their high population of slaves, absolutely refused to arm black men. South Carolina called out its militia to prevent slave uprisings. Virginia, however, allowed free blacks to enlist. Many of these enlistees became Navy seamen.

During the summer of 1775, General George Washington and the other military leaders, stationed outside of Boston, were trying to turn farmers, carpenters, blacksmiths, and laborers into professional soldiers, so that they could recapture Boston, then held by British troops. In July, though, the leaders of the newly formed Continental Army sent out orders to its recruiting officers to exclude blacks. The officers were ordered not to enlist "any deserter from the Ministerial army, nor any stroller, Negro, or vagabond."[2]

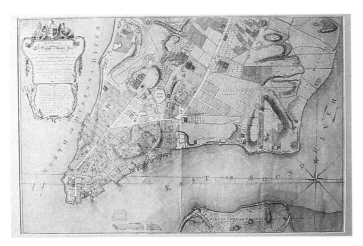

Plan of New York in 1766–67, as drawn by Ratzer. *Courtesy of New York Public Library.*

Some recruiting officers in the New England colonies and in Virginia ignored these orders, and continued to accept free blacks. A number of enslaved men claimed to be free and enlisted, too; however, the British occupying Boston had begun to employ blacks. And the governor of Virginia, Lord Dunmore, had a plan that would throw the Americans into a tailspin. In November, he issued the following proclamation:

"I do hereby . . . declare all indented [sic] servants, Negroes, or others, free, that are able and willing to bear arms, they joining His Majesty's Troops."[3]

Enslaved people in all of the colonies now had a powerful weapon. If they fought for the British, they would be freed. The Americans were outraged, especially in the South, where blacks often outnumbered whites and where the planters would have suffered financial ruin without their enslaved laborers.

When they could, slaves tried to escape to the British fleet in the James River in Virginia after Dunmore's proclamation. They weren't always successful. If they were recaptured, they were either returned to their owners or sold to the colony and made to work in the lead mines, or perform other labor.[4]

As the fighting continued, the enslaved population used military service on both sides of the conflict to gain their own freedom.

The British willingness to offer freedom to blacks in exchange for military service caused the Americans to rethink their policies. As the war continued, recruiting officers in New England, New York, Pennsylvania, and Virginia accepted black volunteers to fill their ranks when white volunteers were hard to find.

In 1778, Rhode Island passed the Enlistment Act. Now, a slave who was qualified physically and mentally for military service would be freed. Rhode Island formed two battalions of former slaves. South Carolina and Georgia, however, continued to refuse to employ black troops.

The recruiters and other military officials recognized that they had a powerful resource in the black population. In December 1775, some Massachusetts officers signed a petition commending a man named Salem Poor. The petition declared that, in the battle at Charlestown,

LIST OF BLACKS WHO SERVED IN REVOLUTIONARY WAR BATTLES IN THE NEW YORK CITY AREA

Name	Battle(s)
Peter Bonet	Stony Point
Bristol Budd	Stony Point
Henry Cato	White Plains
Julius Cezar	Long Island
	Stony Point
York Champlain	White Plains
London Citizen	Long Island
Samuel Dunbar	White Plains
Artillo Freeman	White Plains
Enoch Freeman	Harlem Heights
	White Plains
Primus Hall	Harlem Heights
	White Plains
James Keeter	Harlem Heights
	Kingsbridge
John Francis	Kingsbridge
Pompey Lamb	Stony Point
Salem Poor	White Plains
Timothy Prince	Harlem Heights
	Kingsbridge
	Long Island
Philip Rodman	White Plains
Peter Salem	Stony Point
Caeser Shelton	White Plains
Samuel Sutphin	Long Island
Primus Tyng	Stony Point

New York City Bicentennial Corporation Sub-Committee on Black Contributions.
Ebony Patriots: Participation of Blacks in the Battles of the American Revolution in the New York City area, 1776–1779. New York: The Sub-Committee. 1976.

in Massachusetts, Salem Poor "behaved like an experienced officer, as well as an excellent soldier." The petition went on to say that "in the person of this said [N]egro centers a brave and gallant soldier." Salem Poor also fought later on in the war at Valley Forge, Pennsylvania, and at White Plains, New York.[5]

Other brave and gallant black soldiers and sailors fought on both sides in the Revolution. Burial #6, discussed in Chapter 2, may have been one of them. The British Navy made extensive use of black seamen because of their knowledge of American waterways.

We can only speculate about Burial #6. He may have been one of those men who escaped to the British ships on the James River. Perhaps he had escaped from a plantation in Savannah, Georgia, when British troops occupied that city. Maybe he had been a harbor pilot in Charleston, South Carolina, and joined the British fleet there. Or, he could have joined the navy when British troops captured New York City in 1776.

Ignatio Sanchez, a prominent free black in the British Navy during the Revolutionary War, as painted by T. Gainsborough. *Courtesy of the National Gallery of Canada, Ottawa.*

This piece of coral recovered from the burial of an adult male may signify either African funeral practices or that the individual was a sailor. Seamen were often buried with coral, shells, and other mementos of the sea. *Doville Nelson, photographer. Courtesy of General Services Administration.*

CHAPTER 12

GIVE ME LIBERTY

In the spring of 1776, British troops left Boston with about one thousand American colonists who did not want to break away from Britain. These loyalists set out with the army for New York City. Capturing New York and controlling traffic on the Hudson River would separate the colonies. When the troops abandoned Boston, New York City prepared for the coming invasion.

On March 14, 1776, all black males, slave and free, were ordered to the city Commons. They were told to bring their shovels, pick axes, and other tools

Old City Hall at the time of the American Revolution, from a drawing by David Grim. *From Valentine,* Manual, *1856. Courtesy of New-York Historical Society.*

with them in order to begin building defenses for the city.

As the men gathered in the Commons, just south of the burial ground, some of them might have remembered the events of 1741 and the executions that followed.

Across the bay in Brooklyn, half of the white male population, along with all of the black males, began building fortifications also.[1]

Contrary to the military's orders of 1775, on March 17, 1776, eleven black men were included in Captain Benjamin Egbert's company of fifty-nine men.[2]

Tension and excitement must have run high on the streets of the city as people awaited the coming invasion. Even before the troops came, loyalists were probably trickling into town along with their slaves. It was common during the war for people who remained loyal to the British to move into cities targeted for British occupation.

The establishment of black organizations are reflected in these cufflinks, which may represent a military or fraternal order. Several men were found to be buried with the same type of cufflink.

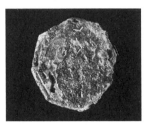

A cufflink found near the throat area of an adult individual in an excavated burial. The design motif is similar to that used by the Freemasons. *Both images, Doville Nelson, photographer. Courtesy of General Services Administration.*

There were also a number of New Yorkers who had always remained loyal to the British empire who were probably secretly overjoyed that the British were coming. The black population by this time also knew about Lord Dunmore's offer of freedom in exchange for military service.

In the shipyards and tanneries, in the bakeries and the pottery shops, in the taverns and at the tea pump, at the pond where black women and poor white women laundered clothing, in the taverns and in the homes, the topics of conversation were surely the same: the war, the British, and Lord Dunmore.

The *New York Journal* printed a poem about Dunmore's policies on May 25, 1776.

> Hail! doughty Ethiopian Chief!
> Though ignominious Negro Thief!
> This Black shall prop thy sinking name,
> And damn thee to perpetual fame.

Another newspaper editor claimed that a black mother in New York City named her newborn child Lord Dunmore.[3] This may have been an exaggeration or an outright lie; however, many blacks in New York were prepared to accept Lord Dunmore's offer.

On July 27, 1776, British troops landed on Staten Island in New York. George Washington had seventeen thousand soldiers ready to defend the city, and on August 27 the siege of New York began in Brooklyn Heights. By November, Fort Washington in the northern hills of Manhattan had capitulated and General Washington had retreated across the Hudson River to New Jersey and then across the Delaware River to Pennsylvania.

By the time winter arrived, General Howe, the British commander, was settled into the Beekman Mansion, his elegant winter quarters in New York City near present-day Fifty-first Street and the East River.[4]

The Christmas season was upon them and the general and his staff enjoyed the holidays. There were parties and social occasions. Business boomed as soldiers frequented the numerous taverns and inns.

Both armies dug in for the winter, and prepared to resume fighting

British in New York during the American Revolution. Here, troops stand in front of the Rhinelander Sugar House, built in 1763. It was used as a prison during the British occupation. *From* The New York Traveler, *volume 4, number 158 (May 1, 1861). Courtesy of New-York Historical Society.*

in the spring. The British occupied New York City for the duration of the war, almost seven years. The city had its share of suffering during occupation. In September 1776, a fire destroyed Trinity Church and many homes. Another fire in 1778 leveled more buildings. Churches were turned into prisons and hospitals.

Now, black New Yorkers who wanted to leave their American masters did not have to take a risky trip across a Virginia river or attempt a dangerous escape from a South Carolina plantation. There were probably women, too, who freed themselves on the way to the tea pump to collect water or to the market to purchase vegetables, by taking themselves to one of the comfortable homes used by British officers and offering their services as cook, laundress, or seamstress.

Freedom could be as near as a short walk to the Commons, where the soldiers' barracks were being built. A strong man could easily offer his services to the British military.

The poorhouse, the jail, and other public buildings on the Commons were now holding American prisoners of war. Many of the prisoners died from disease, hunger, and exposure to the elements. Laborers were always needed to bury the dead. These prisoners were buried in the nearby African Burial Ground, and in churchyards around the city.

The British offer of freedom had its limits, however. The army only freed slaves who had run away from American patriots. They did not free men and women belonging to loyalists. Enslaved people belonging to Americans still loyal to the British were also part of the labor force in occupied New York.

The British offered freedom to all able-bodied men who could be of use to the military, not because they wanted to emancipate blacks, but because it was a way to obtain much-needed manpower, and to deprive the Americans of valuable workers, especially in the South.

In New York City, most of the men who drove the horses, wagons, and carriages carrying military supplies for the quartermaster's department were fugitive slaves working for wages.[5]

The war ended in October 1781. What would happen now to the people who had freed themselves by joining the British military? A year later, when British troops evacuated Charleston, South Carolina, 5,327 formerly enslaved people left with them. Half of them were taken to Jamaica, the rest went to East Florida, which then belonged to England, and some came to New York.[6]

When New York was evacuated in 1783, 3,000 black people boarded the transport ships—1,336 men, 914 women, and 750 children sailed out of the city on British vessels. Most of them went to the Caribbean or Canada.[7] They faced an uncertain future. But they had finally won a valuable piece of property—themselves.

CHAPTER 13

OUT OF MANY, ONE PEOPLE

After the war, the African Burial Ground was becoming over-crowded, like all of the other cemeteries in the city. A new potter's field was opened near the poorhouse; however, people of color were still interred in the African Burial Ground. That would not change for a while.

For enslaved people, it seemed as though nothing had changed. Even if not strictly enforced, the slave laws were still in effect in New York City. If there were any black people who followed the old traditions and decided to have a night funeral, they'd be committing a crime. If three or more enslaved people met, for anything other than work, they'd also be breaking the law.

Many blacks, especially those who sincerely believed in the patriots' cause, were disgusted and disillusioned, but their spirits were unbroken. When America's founding fathers unleashed the powerful words of the Declaration of Independence, "All men are created equal," the words became the property of everyone who heard and understood.

No matter what others might have thought of them, blacks knew that they were men and women entitled to "life, liberty and the pursuit of happiness."

In all of their struggles, from the time of Paolo d'Angola, Manuel de Gerritt, Simon Congo, and the other Africans who petitioned the Dutch West India Company for their freedom, to the brave but ill-fated attempts at revolt, blacks in New York had been hammering away at the chains that bound them. In the decades after the end of the Revolution, those chains would be weakened and finally discarded.

One of the main reasons for the erosion of the slave system in New York City was the growing population of free blacks. There were thousands of black men throughout all of the former colonies who were freed after serving in the Continental Army. Many of them purchased their wives' and their children's freedom.

There were also people in New York who'd escaped from plantation slavery. They had come to the city with the British forces, and remained when the war was over. They lived, however, with the constant threat that a former owner would claim them, for they were still considered property.

In 1784 New York State passed a law freeing the slaves of loyalists who'd left the city with the British. The state banned slave trading in 1786 and again in 1788.

Economic considerations had the greatest effect on the slave system. Immigration increased after the war, and the growing pool of available white laborers made it cheaper to hire a worker for low wages than to maintain an enslaved man or woman from birth to death.

In the spirit of the Revolution, a number of people freed slaves during this period. Some slaveholders may have felt guilty, for, no matter how much slave owners tried to justify slavery, it would continue to tarnish American democratic ideals. New York City records show few certificates of manumission being filed before the 1790s—only twenty-nine between the years 1708 and 1797. In a twenty-two-year period, from 1797 to 1819, 771 certificates of manumission were filed at the Office of the Register of New York.[1]

On February 26, 1800, John Merrit agreed to free his slave, Mary, "after she pays him 40 pounds."

Henry Smith, Esq., freed Samuel Jackson, age forty. He also freed Jackson's son, Francis. In his papers filed on May 6, 1799, Smith says he is freeing Francis who is four years and five months old, because of the "fidelity and past services of his father."

Owner Thomas Behenna, filed manumission papers on January 21, 1753, stating that Molle and her daughter, Jenny, would be freed only after his death.

Thomas Tillotson filed papers on May 16, 1797, acknowledging that he had received twenty pounds from a black woman named Sarah, who was purchasing her daughter, Sukey, from Tillotson. Tillotson promised to free her if Sukey performed "her services faithfully," until January 21, 1799.

Thomas Charnock, carpenter, and a free black man, purchased his son George, age 16, for $400 from Isaac Edwards of Charleston, South Carolina, on November 23, 1809. He probably filed manumission papers in New York, on September 12, 1813, in order to protect George's freedom. Charnock eloquently states that he had "to release from the galling chains of slavery (the base as well as the disgrace of a free Country) and to liberate, manumit and set free the said George. . . ." He goes on to describe his son as "well educated in the Arts and Sciences in the City of New York."[2]

George Washington was among those who freed their slaves. Mary Simpson served the general during his stay in New York. She took in laundry to support herself and ran a small store where she sold pies, cakes, and sweetmeats. Every year at her home on what is now Nassau and Gold streets in lower Manhattan, she celebrated Washington's birthday by baking a gigantic cake and serving coffee and punch. As she served her visitors, she displayed a small trunk with Washington's initials and his portrait, both gifts from him. Her Washington birthday celebration became an annual New York City event.[3] Mary Simpson held her celebration until she died in 1836. She was afraid that if she didn't celebrate Washington's birthday, he "would soon be forgotten."[4]

In addition to individual manumissions, a group of prominent New Yorkers, including John Jay and Alexander Hamilton, organized the Manumission Society on January 2, 1785. When the society opened African Free School No. 1 on William Street in 1786, forty boys and girls were there to receive free instruction in reading, writing, and domestic and manual training, including navigation.[5]

As the numbers of free people rose and opportunities for education opened, people who remained enslaved gained strength from their free brethren. In many cases, both groups were barely distinguishable from one another. Freed blacks had few political and civil rights. They could not vote and they could not hold political office.

The more the free population grew, the more they were limited in the types of employment they could obtain. Black men who were skilled artisans when they were enslaved could no longer hold those jobs, which were now reserved for the rising population of white laborers.

Some people, though, managed to climb over the high walls of racism and prejudice. Pierre Toussaint came to New York from Santo Domingo in 1787 with his owners, Jean Berard and his wife. The Berards were French planters in Santo Domingo, and settled into the French community in New York. Pierre, a hairdresser, became very popular among well-to-do New York ladies. Though he was enslaved, he kept a portion of the money he earned and managed to accumulate some savings.

When Jean Berard did not return from a business trip to Santo Domingo, Pierre Toussaint supported and cared for Berard's wife with his earnings. Toussaint was freed when Madame Berard died. Toussaint's generosity did not end when he himself became free. No doubt, in his mind, he was always free. The affluent hairdresser helped many others. He bought his niece's freedom and in 1811 he purchased the freedom of his future wife.

Pierre Toussaint was a devout Catholic who gave to many benevolent causes throughout his lifetime. He contributed money for the construction of a Catholic church, and gave funds regularly to the Catholic Orphan Asylum, an orphanage for white children. He also purchased the freedom of many young black men.

PIERRE TOUSSAINT
1766–1853

Pierre Toussaint. *Courtesy of the Catholic Archdiocese of New York.*

Toussaint died at the age of eighty-seven and is buried in St. Patrick's Cemetery on present-day Mott Street, near where the black-owned farms once stood.[6]

Few blacks in those years had the wealth of a Toussaint. Often free African Americans were not much better off than those who were enslaved. But in those post–Revolutionary War years, both groups had a common cause and were beginning to speak with one voice.

In 1788 free and enslaved blacks filed a petition with the Common Council, protesting the desecration of the graves in their burial ground by medical students from a nearby hospital. Students regularly dug up bodies in order to perform autopsies as part of their medical training.

It hath lately been the constant practice of a number of young gentlemen in this city who call themselves students . . .

to repair to the burial ground assigned for the use of your
petitioners and under cover of night . . . to dig up the bodies
of the deceased friends and relatives of your petitioners, carry
them away. . . .[7]

The petitioners may have known of the activities of African
Americans in other northern cities who were seizing control of their
lives, too. In Philadelphia the year before, Richard Allen and Absolom
Jones, along with six other men, founded the Free African Society.
This self-help, black benevolent society would ultimately give birth to
one of the first independent African-American religious denomina-
tions and national organizations: the African Methodist Episcopal
Church.

By 1790 there were 1,011 free and 2,369 enslaved African Americans
living in New York City. Ten years later, the number of free people rose
to 2,868.[8]

The city was stretching its boundaries northward by 1794. Land was
needed for streets and new buildings; however, additional space was
required not only for the living, but for the dead as well. The potter's

Autopsied skull recov-
ered from the burial
ground excavations. This
individual may have
been exhumed by med-
ical students who per-
formed an autopsy and
then reburied the re-
mains. *Dennis Seckler,
photographer. Courtesy
of General Services
Administration.*

field near the old Revolutionary War barracks and poorhouse was full, and the city had to find another site for a paupers' cemetery. When a new site was found near present-day Madison Square Garden, a New York paper wrote: "The new ground is to be planted with trees. It would be desirable that the measure should lead to a general removal of burial grounds from the center of the city."[9] The article foreshadowed the end of the African Burial Ground. It also foretold the end of an era.

The African Burial Ground was the final resting place for people of African descent from many parts of the world. They came from Portugal and Angola, Guinea and Jamaica and Nevis, Barbados and the Bahamas, Charleston and Savannah, Madagascar and Brazil, Santo Domingo and Curaçao. The African Burial Ground held the African diaspora. Out of many, one people.[10]

The African Burial Ground was closed in 1796 when the city began developing the land for new streets and homes. A group of blacks, forming an organization called the African Society, requested land from the city to open a new burial ground for African Americans. They were granted land on Chrystie Street, in today's Lower East Side.

It was a landmark year in the history of black New Yorkers. The African Burial Ground was closed, and a turbulent century was closing as well. But 1796 was also the beginning of an era that would witness the development and growth of one of the most important African-American institutions—the independent black church.

In 1796, Peter Williams received his manumission certificate, though he'd been free since 1785, and was a prosperous tobacconist with his own business. Williams was a religious man. He had worked as a sexton for several years for the Wesley Chapel, today known as the John Street United Methodist Church. The church trustees had purchased Williams from his former owner, John Aymar, when Aymar fled New York in the British evacuation. Williams didn't want to be

Peter Williams, founder of the African Methodist Episcopal Zion Church. *Courtesy of the John Street Methodist Church*

sold away from his family and asked the church trustees to buy him from Aymar. In three years he repaid the church the forty pounds he'd cost them, and was freed.

Peter Williams remained a faithful worshiper at the church. Over one hundred other African Americans worshiped there as well. But in 1796 because of the church's refusal to fully ordain black ministers and other discriminatory practices, Williams and the other black worshipers organized an African chapel in a cabinet-maker's shop owned by one of the black members.

Four years later, they purchased a lot on Church and Leonard streets. In the years to come, they would establish the African Methodist Episcopal Zion Church. Mother A.M.E. Zion Church, the first independent black church in New York City, is one of the most famous churches in Harlem today.

By the 1850's the African Methodist Episcopal Zion Church had a burial ground on today's Eighty-fifth Street between Seventh and Eighth avenues.[11]

In 1808 black members of the First Baptist Church on Gold Street organized the Abyssinian Baptist Church. It, too, remains one of the most important churches in the Harlem community.[12]

And in 1818 black members of Trinity Church and St. Paul's Chapel left their segregated pews and founded St. Philip's Episcopal Church. Peter Williams, Jr., the son of Peter Williams, the first African American to be ordained in the United States, became its pastor. The church erected its first building on Collect Street, now Centre Street. Eventually, St. Philip's Church would operate the burial ground on Chrystie Street. Today, St. Philip's is still holding worship services in Harlem.

The growth and development of independent black denominations and churches in New York City, as well as black communities all over the country, mark the beginning of a people as well. African and American. Mother Zion, Abyssinian Baptist, and the many other independent black churches developing at this time, were not only religious institutions, but were instrumental in the development of African-American leaders and cultural, political, and social values as well.

Freedom's Journal began publishing in 1827 in New York City and was the nation's first African-American newspaper. *Courtesy of New-York Historical Society.*

New York State finally ended slavery in 1827, but racism and prejudice continued. That same year two black men, Samuel Cornish and John Russworm, opened their newspaper offices on Church Street. *Freedom's Journal,* the nation's first black newspaper, would give black New Yorkers a strong, loud voice in the new phase of the struggle for freedom.

The ancestors would, finally, rest in peace.

EPILOGUE

In 1992, when news of the excavation of an eighteenth-century burial ground for people of African descent in New York City spread to the general public, people realized that this was a monumental discovery that would offer us the chance to reclaim a lost history. It makes the past real to us, as we gaze at the remains of a mother and child, or a woman in ceremonial beads, or observe an earbob worn by a little girl. We are made to think and to feel.

As interest in the burial ground grew, especially among African Americans, some voices rose in outrage against further excavation and desecration of the graves. The cruelties these individuals suffered in life should not be repeated after death. People argued that the spiritual significance of the site went even deeper than its scientific and historical value. This was hallowed ground.

A forceful and determined group of black

Some members of the descendant community voiced their objections to the excavations at the burial site. *Cheryl LaRoche, photographer. Courtesy of photographer.*

New Yorkers and others began a campaign to end the excavations and the proposed construction.

In 1788 the City Council ignored a petition from a group of black New Yorkers asking the council to stop the medical students from grave robbing. Fortunately, this was 1992.

The city of New York now had a black mayor, David Dinkins, who understood the historical and cultural significance of the discovery. The mayor appointed a liaison from his office to monitor activities at the site.

With the influence of Congressman Gus Savage, who was chairman of the House Subcommittee on Public Buildings and Grounds, the excavations were halted by the end of July in 1992.

New York State Senator David Patterson formed a steering committee of black activists, journalists, artists, scholars, students, clergy,

Former New York City Mayor David Dinkins and his burial ground task force visit the excavation site. *Dennis Seckler, photographer. Courtesy of General Services Administration.*

and ordinary citizens, all agreeing that the descendant community had to have some control over this important historical site. However, everyone did not agree as to the best way to honor the ancestors and to reclaim the history.

Some people demanded that the office building not be constructed at all. They also wanted the bones that had been excavated to be reinterred. (Initially, the bones were analyzed by forensic specialists to determine things such as the age, sex, and race of the individual. Once the analysis was complete, the bones probably would have been placed in a museum.)

Others felt that since the graves had already been violated and the remains excavated, further studies should be conducted to learn how these individuals might have lived.

Still others believed that this was an extraordinary opportunity to give a people who had been written out of history a voice. Scientists, anthropologists, archaeologists, and historians could combine their skills and the art of their disciplines to recreate this lost history.

The federal agency constructing the building (along with a four-story pavilion to house a day-care center, parking garage, and food court) continued construction. But because of the barrage of community pressure and widespread interest in the site, concessions were made.

Construction plans were altered and the building was completed in 1994. There is a memorial to the African children, women, and men interred in this historic six-acre burial ground.

The excavated remains were transferred to Howard University in Washington, D.C., a historically black university where a team of anthropologists, archaeologists, and historians, headed by Dr. Michael L. Blakey, are analyzing the skeletal remains. The Howard University team, along with the archaeologists at the Foley Square Laboratory in New York City, bring to their work not only their scientific and academic expertise, but also a knowledge of and sensitivity to the culture and history of the people whose remains they are analyzing. After analyses of the remains are completed, they will be re-interred in the African Burial Ground Memorial site.

View of the burial ground site at night. Often, the archaeological crew worked until late in the evening. *Dennis Seckler, photographer. Courtesy of Historic Conservation Interpretation.*

As a result of the determined efforts of many community people to reclaim this history, the Office of Public Education and Interpretation (OPEI) for the African Burial Ground, under the direction of Dr. Sherrill D. Wilson, was established in 1993. OPEI conducts educational tours, school programs, and seminars. Through its newsletter, OPEI has provided information about the burial ground to thousands of people worldwide. Scholars from all over the world, including many African nations, have visited the laboratories in New York and Washington, D.C.

For example, in 1995 members of the National House of Chiefs of Ghana visited the burial ground, where they conducted an atonement and reunification ritual in memory of the thousands of Africans and African descendants interred in the burial ground.

Another moving tribute to the memory of the ancestors and the recovery of our history was the children's art project in 1993. Schoolchildren from around the city interpreted through art their feelings about the African Burial Ground, expressing honestly and sincerely what this past means to them.

It is, in the end, the children who are the most important part of this story. For they will become the men and women who will continue the important work of recovering this history.

Some of them will be the archaeologists, anthropologists, historians, and scientists of the future, continuing to explore and strengthen our ties to the past.

The New York City African Burial Ground and the Commons Historic District were granted landmark status on February 25, 1993, by the New York City Landmarks Commission.

Many men and women of African descent were moved in profound ways by the discovery of the burial ground. Here, a couple with their child renew their ties to a forgotten past. The infant embodies the continuation of life, the rebirth of the ancestors. *Dennis Seckler, photographer. Courtesy of Cheryl LaRoche.*

New York City schoolchildren interpret, through their eloquent art, the history of the African Burial Ground. *Austin Hansen, Sr., photographer. Courtesy of Joyce Hansen.*

The African Burial Ground in New York City received National Historic Landmark status on April 19, 1993. It is the oldest and largest known cemetery for people of African descent in the nation.

At a ceremony to acknowledge and celebrate the African Burial Ground's new status both in New York City and in the United States, Mayor David N. Dinkins made the following remarks:

> Millions of Americans celebrate Ellis Island as the symbol of their communal identity in this land. Others celebrate Plymouth Rock. Until a few years ago, African American New Yorkers had no site to call our own. There was no place which said, we were here, we contributed, we played a significant role in New York's history right from the beginning. . . .
>
> Now we—their descendants—have the symbol of our heritage embodied in lower Manhattan's African Burial Ground. . . . Again and again I have witnessed the power this site has to move people's hearts, and to educate their minds.
>
> And not just the hearts and minds of African Americans. By opening a window into a long forgotten part of New York's past, the Burial Ground has changed the past itself. All New Yorkers are enriched by the gift of history it has bestowed.[1]

NOTES

CHAPTER 3

1. J. Franklin Jameson, ed., *Narratives of New Netherland* (New York: Charles Scribner's Sons, 1909), 227–228.
2. Christopher Moore, "Land of the Blacks," *Seaport*, Vol. XXIX, #3 (1995), 10.
3. Moore, 8–11.

CHAPTER 4

1. J. Franklin Jameson, ed., *Narratives of New Netherland* (New York: Charles Scribner's Sons, 1909), 330.
2. Jameson, 365.
3. Roi Ottley and William J. Weatherby, eds., *The Negro in New York* (New York: New York Public Library, 1967), 4.
4. Ottley and Weatherby, 8.
5. Christopher Moore, "Land of the Blacks," *Seaport*, Vol. XXIX, #3 (1995), 11.
6. Jameson, 407.

CHAPTER 5

1. J. Franklin Jameson, ed., *Narratives of New Netherland* (New York: Charles Scribner's Sons, 1909), 408.
2. Roi Ottley and William J. Weatherby, eds., *The Negro in New York* (New York: New York Public Library, 1967), 17.
3. Joyce D. Goodfriend, *Before the Melting Pot* (Princeton, N.J.: Princeton University Press, 1992), 112.
4. David T. Valentine, "History of Broadway," *Manual of the Common Council of New York* (New York: D.T. Valentine, 1865), 567.
5. Robert W. Habenstein and William M. Lamers, *Funeral Customs the World Over* (Milwaukee: The National Funeral Directors Association of the United States, 1994), 219.

CHAPTER 6

1. Cheryl J. LaRoche, "Beads From The African Burial Ground, New York City: A Preliminary Assessment," *Journal of the Society of Bead Researchers,* Vol. 6, (1994), 7.
2. LaRoche, 13–14.
3. LaRoche, 11, 15.
4. LaRoche, 12.
5. James G. Lydon, "New York and the Slave Trade, 1700 to 1774, *William and Mary Quarterly* 35 (1978), 383.
6. The Asante, Fanti, and Akwapim are Akan-speaking peoples in present-day Ghana in West Africa. Professor Asare Kofi Opoku of Lafayette College says that in this culture, blue is the color of love and a spouse will bury his or her loved one with blue beads.
7. Lydon, 377.
8. *The African Burial Ground: An American Discovery*, prod. and dir. David Kutz, assoc. prod. and writer Christopher Moore, 2 hours, U.S. General Services Administration, 1994, videocassette.
9. Kutz, *The African Burial Ground: An American Discovery* (videocassette).
10. Lydon, 377.

CHAPTER 7

1. Roi Ottley and William J. Weatherby, eds., *The Negro in New York* (New York: New York Public Library, 1967), 23.
2. James Weldon Johnson, *Black Manhattan* (Reprint, Salem: Ayer Publishing Company, 1990), 7–8.
3. Joyce D. Goodfriend, *Before the Melting Pot: Society and Culture in Colonial New York 1664–1730* (Princeton N.J.: Princeton University Press, 1992), 124.
4. Rhoda Golden Freeman, *The Free Negro in New York City in the Era Before the Civil War* (New York: Garland Publishing, Inc., 1994), 8.
5. Johnson, 7.
6. Goodfriend, 116.

CHAPTER 8

1. Thomas J. Davis, *A Rumor of Revolt: The "Great Negro Plot" in Colonial New York.* (Amherst: The University of Massachusetts Press, 1990), 32.
2. Joyce D. Goodfriend, *Before the Melting Pot: Society and Culture in Colonial New York 1664–1730* (Princeton: Princeton University Press, 1992), 119.
3. James G. Lydon, "New York and the Slave Trade, 1700 to 1774," *William and Mary Quarterly* 35 (1978), 393.
4. Goodfriend, 124.
5. Goodfriend, 119.
6. Goodfriend, 120.
7. Davis, 51–52.
8. Daniel Horsmanden, *The New York Conspiracy:* (New York: Southwick & Pelsue, 1810; Reprint, Boston: Beacon Press, 1971), 56–57.

CHAPTER 9

1. David Grim, 1813, as quoted in "Overlooking The Collect," Christopher P. Neville unpublished manuscript, Columbia University, 1994.
2. Daniel Horsmanden, *The New York Conspiracy* (Reprint, Boston: Beacon Press, 1971), 387–388.
3. Horsmanden, 397.
4. Horsmanden, 411, 413.
5. James Weldon Johnson, *Black Manhattan* (Reprint, Salem: Ayer Publishing Company, 1990), 10.
6. Thomas J. Davis, *A Rumor of Revolt: The "Great Negro Plot" in Colonial New York.* (Amherst: The University of Massachusetts Press, 1990), 252.
7. James G. Lydon, "New York and the Slave Trade, 1700 to 1774," *William and Mary Quarterly* 35 (1978), 393.

CHAPTER 10

1. Mark E. Mack, "Dental Observations of the New York Burial Ground Skeletal Population." Notes from the Howard University Biological Anthropology Laboratory. Newsletter of the African Burial Ground & Five Points Archaeological Projects, Vol. 1, No. 6 (1995), 4.
2. Mark E. Mack and M. Cassandra Hill, "Pathologies Affecting Children in the African Burial Ground Population," Newsletter of the African Burial Ground & Five Points Archaeological Projects, Vol. 1, No. 7 (1995), 4.
3. Mark E. Mack, "Recent Research Findings Concerning the African Burial Ground Population." Newsletter of the African Burial Ground, Vol. 1, No. 9 (1995), 3–4.

CHAPTER 11

1. Benjamin Quarles, *The Negro in the American Revolution* (Chapel Hill: The University of North Carolina Press, 1991), 10.
2. Quarles, 15.
3. Quarles, 19.
4. Quarles, 23.
5. Quarles, 11.

CHAPTER 12

1. Benjamin Quarles, *The Negro in the American Revolution* (Chapel Hill: The University of North Carolina Press. 1991), 98.
2. Quarles, 12.
3. Quarles, 31.
4. Gene Schermerhorn, *Letters to Phil: Memories of a New York Boyhood, 1848–1856* (New York: New York Bound, 1982), 42.
5. Quarles, 134.
6. Quarles, 167.
7. Quarles, 172.
For fascinating information about

freed men, women, and children who left with the British in 1783, see Graham Russell Hodges, *The Black Loyalist Directory* (New York: Garland Publishing, Inc. 1996).

CHAPTER 13

1. Rhoda Golden Freeman, *The Free Negro in New York City in the Era Before the Civil War* (New York: Garland Publishing, Inc., 1994), 6.
2. Harry B. Yoshpe, Ph.D., "Record of Slave Manumissions in New York During the Colonial and Early National Periods," *Journal of Negro History* (Vol. 26, 1941), 78–107.
3. M.A. Harris, *A Negro History Tour of Manhattan* (New York: Greenwood Publishing, 1968), 23.
4. Roi Ottley and William J. Weatherby, eds., *The Negro in New York* (New York: New York Public Library 1967), 38–39.
5. Ottley and Weatherby, 63.
6. Ottley and Weatherby, 65–67.
7. Phelps Stokes, *Iconography of Manhattan Island,* quoted in *Over-looking the Collect: Between Topography and Memory in the Landscape of Lower Manhattan,* Christopher P. Neville (Graduate School of Architecture, Planning and Preservation, Columbia University, 1994), 54.
8. Freeman, 6.
9. Neville, 56.
10. Motto on the Jamaican national flag. Many of the enslaved men and women coming to colonial New York were from the British colony of Jamaica, today an independent Caribbean nation.
11. Harris, 42. Also C. Eric Lincoln and Lawrence H. Mamiya, *The Black Church in the African American Experience* (Durham: Duke University Press, 1990), 56.
12. Harris, 21–22.

EPILOGUE

1. Edward Kaufman, ed., *Reclaiming Our Past, Honoring Our Ancestors,* (New York: The African Burial Ground Competition Coalition, 1994), 1.

BIBLIOGRAPHY

Davis, Thomas J. *A Rumor of Revolt: The "Great Negro Plot" in Colonial New York*. Amherst: The University of Massachusetts Press, 1990.

Freeman, Rhoda Golden. *The Free Negro in New York City in the Era Before the Civil War*. New York: Garland Publishing, Inc., 1994.

Goodfriend, Joyce D. *Before the Melting Pot: Society and Culture in Colonial New York 1664–1730*. Princeton, N.J.: Princeton University Press, 1992.

Harris, M.A. *A Negro History Tour of Manhattan*. New York: Greenwood Publishing, 1968.

Homberger, Eric. *The Historical Atlas of New York City*. New York: Henry Holt and Company, 1994.

Horsmanden, Daniel. *The New York Conspiracy*. New York: Southwick & Pelsue, 1810; Reprint, Boston: Beacon Press, 1971.

Jameson, J. Franklin, ed. *Narratives of New Netherland*. New York: Charles Scribner's Sons, 1909.

Johnson, James Weldon. *Black Manhattan*. Reprint, Salem: Ayer Publishing Company, 1990.

Lincoln, C. Eric, and Lawrence H. Mamiya. *The Black Church in the African American Experience*. Durham, N.C.: Duke University Press, 1990.

Middleton, Richard. *Colonial America*. Cambridge & Oxford: Blackwell, 1992.

Ottley, Roi, and William J. Weatherby, eds. *The Negro in New York*. New York: New York Public Library, 1967.

Quarles, Benjamin. *The Negro in the American Revolution*. Chapel Hill: The University of North Carolina Press, 1991.

INDEX

Page numbers in *italics* refer to illustrations and captions.